BE YOUR
BEST
SELF

BE YOUR
BEST
SELF

AN INTERACTIVE
COMPANION

MIKE BAYER

DEY ST.
An Imprint of WILLIAM MORROW

DEY ST.

HarperCollins books may be purchased for educational, business, or sales promotional use. For information, please email the Special Markets Department at SPsales@harpercollins.com.

FIRST EDITION

Library of Congress Cataloging-in-Publication Data has been applied for.

ISBN 978-0-06-300159-6

20 21 22 23 24 LSC 10 9 8 7 6 5 4 3 2 1

Contents

Introduction

Who are you?

We rarely, if ever, slow down enough in our lives to really ask ourselves that question. But that is the central goal of this workbook—to take the time, do the work, and have the reward of discovering what makes you uniquely you.

One of the observations I've made over two decades of working with people is that our external world will match how aligned we are with our authentic self. For example, if you don't believe you are worthy of having close, true friends, you will isolate yourself a lot in your social life. This will prevent you from having those meaningful friendships. Or if you have low self-esteem, you will create a life in which you are surrounded by people and things that validate your low opinion. In other words, however you feel internally will be mirrored externally, because of your choices, whether conscious or subconscious.

Our society likes to focus on hugely popular celebrities who seem like they "have it all," who are wildly successful and wealthy, travel all over the world, and live what seem to be amazing lives. The reality is that many of these people are totally miserable inside. We've all heard those stories, and they seem so unbelievable from an outside perspective. "How could he/she be depressed and suicidal? He's got millions in the bank, and international fame!" But, let's reframe that question in terms of the external environment matching our internal beliefs I just discussed. If you were to peel back the layers of glitz and glamour and really see that person's life up close, what you might discover is that his or her immediate surroundings and their day-to-day existence perpetuate their misery. In other words, they spend time engaging in unhealthy behaviors, people, places, and things. And it's all because of one big problem—he or she isn't aligned with their authentic self, their Best Self. No amount of material, external success can ever solve that problem. You have to dig deep and identify your Best Self within, and create the life that honors that version of yourself.

On the other hand, consider the person who is just getting by, but who leaps out of bed in the morning, feeling off-the-charts content and happy with their life because they are living each day as his or her Best Self. Perhaps he or she takes time to experience the power of gratitude, to stay intimately connected with loved ones, to give back to the community, and to maintain self-care and an emotional balance. Cultivating this kind of authentic life does not require monetary wealth, perfect physical health, or anything other than a commitment to live as our Best Self. The point is this: we create our reality, and what the world sees when they look at us is *far* from the whole story. If there was a news story about you today, it wouldn't be the whole story. Right? That would be impossible to capture. Others would have no idea what's really going on in your life or in your head. Only *you* can know if you are choosing to live as your Best Self so that you can squeeze every last drop of vitality, love, and inspiration out of this life, and only you can know what is holding you back if you aren't.

This is the workbook/companion guide to *Best Self: Be You, Only Better.* In my first book, I wanted to help readers clearly define, deeply connect with, and learn to live each day as their Best Self. I knew from all of the thousands of hours I'd spent working with people across every imaginable walk of life, dealing with an extremely wide range of obstacles, that most issues in life come from a lack of connection with our authenticity. I believed if I could just help folks get to know who they are at their core, that they would then hold the key to creating a life they'd only ever dreamed of. I was feeling exhilarated when the book went to print because I knew that if only one person's life improved as a result of what I'd written, then it was a total win. But I could never have predicted the unique and compelling stories of transformation that have poured in from around the world on my Facebook and Instagram platforms. I continue to be deeply humbled and honored by the results. My mission has always been to help people discover the freedom to be the best version of themselves, and I've now communicated with thousands of people who feel they've done just that as a result of the work they did in *Best Self*. Notice I said the work *they* did. I didn't do the work for them and I can't do it for you, but we can do it together. And that's exactly why I wanted to create this companion. When I reviewed *Best Self*, I saw opportunities to go further into the concepts so that you can unlock more truths about yourself and find new applications for the wisdom you've gained. Yes, it would be helpful for you to read that book first, but it's not required in order to use the exercises in this workbook. What *is* required is for you to be curious, open, honest, willing, and focused to go on this journey.

I want to help you discover exactly how you can **be you, only better**, in order to feel fully equipped for navigating anything and everything that happens in life. We can't ever predict what's coming our way, but we can choose to live authentically so that we are actively creating a life we want, and that matches our intentions. If you follow "Coach Mike Bayer" on any of my social media platforms, which I encourage you to do, then you'll see that I share positive content meant to help you accomplish just this and how I strive to do the same.

If right now, you're thinking, "Yeah, but I don't have time," or, "Yeah, but I have so much baggage from my past," or, "Yeah, but my circumstances are too complicated," then I would say this—I'm not here to convince you. If you're a "yeah, but . . ." person, then I can't help you. You can either choose to live in your rut, your anger, or your pain or you can choose to turn your negativity into inspiration. But openness is an essential ingredient in this recipe for authentic living. The more open you are to the possibilities and to the process, the more opportunities you'll uncover.

So, before you can start to really sync up your life with who you are, you need to get to know yourself. I'll break the ice right now and share with you how I see myself. I am a spirit who is fun, clever, artistic, out-of-the-box, determined, resilient, and ever-evolving. That's who I am, and importantly, that's who *I tell myself* I am. Because who you are can't be based upon other people's perceptions of you—you are in charge of your own narrative.

I love how resilient I am. Of course, I don't love going through difficulty, but I know I have a choice—if something bad happens, I can choose to wallow and get stuck, or I can say to myself, "Okay, I will accept this and I will live in this for right now. And then I am going to find inspiration, and I am going to move through it and grow from it." The latter is the choice I make. That, I believe, is resiliency. It's one of a multitude of topics I often dive into with guests on *The Coach Mike Podcast*, and I invite you to listen and hear for yourself some of the fascinating conversations I've had with folks from many industries and parts of the world. I've loved having the opportunity to delve into the human psyche and our extraordinary capacity to live as our Best Self with people who have beaten the odds, risen above their circumstances, pivoted into new and unexpected directions, or reinvented their lives from the inside out. Overhaulers, underdogs, superstars, up-and-comers, way-makers, and trailblazers alike . . . they all have a story, and they are all powered by an authenticity battery, just like you and me. We have so much to learn from one another's journeys, and I am thrilled to offer a platform for sharing those stories and insights.

When we think about "who we are," often we say things like "I'm a mom," "I'm a daughter," "I'm a sister," "I'm a son," which are all aspects of someone's life, but they are roles we play relative to someone *else*. Being a son does not define who I am as a spirit. Yes, I'm a son, but only until I don't have parents anymore. I am a son only in relation to my parents. It is still important, as are all the roles we play, certainly. But it is not the essence of me, the core of my authentic self. Through the exploration you'll do within this book, I hope you will be able to figure out who you are on the most essential, soulful level.

I find that most people only think about who they really are when they are feeling stuck in some aspect of life. Why wait until there's a problem? Why not take the time now to cultivate and create a rich understanding of yourself? I think of this as your Best Self life guidebook. The work you'll be doing here, should you be willing and curious enough to do it, is more important than any workbook you ever completed in school. And no textbook was ever written that contained information superior to what you could potentially learn here. Why? Because this book is about *you*. It's about discovering your truth, becoming your Best Self, and then living the life you were meant to live.

The first time I encountered a workbook that meant something to me on the level that this one could mean to you was when I was beginning my journey toward getting sober. I dug into every single exercise, allowed myself to be completely vulnerable in my answers, and made it my top priority above all else. I knew I didn't want to go back to the half-life I had been leading. I saw each page I completed in the workbook as another step out of that darkness. Before you ask, no, this is not a "rehab" workbook. It is not designed solely or even specifically for those who are working toward freedom from the stranglehold of addiction. This is a guide that can reveal answers to questions you haven't even known to ask, and regardless of where you're starting from, it can take you where you've always wanted to go. Bottom line— if you're looking to relaunch, rediscover, or reinvent any aspect of your life, then this workbook can be your springboard. But you only get out of it what you put in.

This process doesn't have to be arduous. In fact, you should fully expect to have some laugh-out-loud moments while you're exploring this book. Change can, and should, be fun! Figuring out what makes us tick, and connecting dots we've never seen before, is exhilarating. Yes, you have to dig up the past and closely examine your present, but envisioning a greater future is powerful. This journey is about opening up new channels of our imagination. It's about uncovering our hidden talents, desires, and needs and activating them to improve our lives.

In *Best Self* the book, the very first exercise is to design your own Best Self. You describe him or her in great detail, and even draw a picture. Before you start this companion guide, return to that exercise and transfer your own Best Self onto this page, or, do it here for the first time. Get creative, and get out your art supplies.

My Best Self's name is: _____

_____

I describe my Best Self as: _____

_____

_____

This is what my Best Self looks like:

The way I've organized this companion guide is by the seven SPHERES of life (Social, Personal, Health, Education, Relationship, Employment, Spiritual). Together, we are going to delve deeper into each area of your life so that you can more completely connect and sync up your Best Self within those SPHERES. You may already know which of your SPHERES are the most out of balance, as evidenced by issues you're having in specific parts of your life. I've found that to be true in the Best Self Coaching Group on Facebook, for sure—most folks know right off the bat which are the most troublesome SPHERES for them. You may, of course, begin your work within the SPHERES that most urgently require your attention. Or you can work through this workbook in order. The choice is yours. We all behave differently in different settings, but if you are acting in a way that runs contrary to who you are authentically in a particular area of your life and that feels uncomfortable, that's an indication that you might be out of balance in that area. If that is the case, I urge you to focus there first. But, again, what you get out of this workbook is what you put into it. The idea is to build upon the work you did in *Best Self*, and find new ways that you can feel aligned with your passions and authenticity.

The most important thing to keep in mind as you progress is to approach each exercise in this book as your Best Self. If you did the work in the book, then you are familiar with your Best Self and your Anti-Self. All of us have at least one Anti-Self—that side of ourselves that is driven by ego, fear, and other negative forces. It has nothing to do with who we really are, but certain triggers can cause us to slip into old habits or thought patterns that don't serve us. If you begin to feel your Anti-Self sneaking in or trying to take over, take a moment to center yourself. For me, when that begins to happen, one of the ways I can most quickly wrestle my Anti-Self down is to write about it. What triggered this? What feelings did I experience that might have brought my Anti-Self to the forefront? How do I push him away? One of my Anti-Selves is named Angelos—I think of him as a male witch. He isolates, lacks inspiration, lacks purpose, and blames others for how he feels. The more I can analyze and understand the mechanics of Angelos's appearance, the less likely he is to return. Then, once you've reframed your thinking, continue onward.

I don't know your level of willingness at this moment in time when it comes to peeling back your personal layers. I don't know if you see it as your life hanging in the balance like I did when I was getting sober—like the discoveries you make in this process could be transformational—or if you're just a casual observer, flipping through the pages of this book with the vague indifference of someone who hasn't given too much thought to your quality of life because you're so focused on day-to-day responsibilities. You likely fall somewhere in between, but either way, I know, deep in my soul, that you have the potential to live the best possible version of the life you have on this earth as your Best Self. And unless you can honestly say that you're already doing that, then there's something in this book for you. It might be a big something. It might be that you've unknowingly been sleepwalking through your life, and this is your alarm—because it's time to wake up, to rise up, and to transcend the monotony of a life of chasing the wind. It's time to discover your place, your calling, and the truth about who you really are.

Let's get going. Your new reality awaits.

Be Your Best "Social" Self

In order to socialize from a place of authenticity, you
have to be willing to be in the moment with others.
—*Best Self*

I n this chapter, the core question you're going to be asking is "Am I living an authentic social life?" Our social life has to do with how we relate to others in our life, how effectively we communicate our messages. As you turn your attention to your Social SPHERE, think about whether this is an area that helps you be the best version of yourself, and supports you in those efforts, or if it is an area causing you stress and anxiety, maybe even to the point that you isolate and choose not to engage with others. Likely the answer lies somewhere in between, but it's important that you take the time to explore the current state of your social life, and then determine what's working and what isn't. Especially in today's world, when much of our "social" life actually takes place when we are physically isolated from one another, via social media, it's perhaps easier for us to get out of balance and farther away from our own authenticity in this SPHERE than in any other.

We all navigate different circles of people in our lives. We have connections and confidants at work, at school, and within our families, our "going out" friends, our "staying in" friends, and so on. Are you thriving within some of those circles and just barely surviving in others?

When you are actively socializing with others, do you find yourself struggling to be authentic, just trying to blend in? Or do you feel very much in your element when you're socializing, and able to listen to others attentively while sharing aspects of your true identity with confidence? Maybe you haven't spent much time considering how you come across when you're socializing, as it hasn't been a priority for you. I firmly believe that acting as your Best Self when you're socializing is imperative. Why? Well, when you're with others, you're given a chance to project who you really are out into the world, and we often receive from others that which we are giving. When we see ourselves behaving as our Best Self, we become more connected with our authenticity, and it becomes easier to stay in that state of mind. Then, as others see us being authentic, they are more likely to show up as their Best Self as well. There is so much more freedom in being true to who we are when we're with other people, rather than trying to fit in with the crowd, or shrinking away from socialization altogether. That's why I encourage you to spend some time identifying how skilled you are at behaving as your Best Self in your Social SPHERE, and then working toward effectively honing those skills.

I like to think about the Social SPHERE as being broken into these categories:

How we socialize

- Sending clear messages
- Listening
- Giving and receiving feedback
- Handling emotional interactions

Who we socialize with

- Family
- Colleagues
- School associates
- Friends
- Acquaintances

Fill in any other general groups with which you socialize:

_____

_____

_____

First, get in touch with how you're faring in each of the categories by completing the Social Skills Inventory starting on page 109 in *Best Self.* You can use that valuable insight to discover why you might be struggling in your social life. The four skills listed above really go hand in hand, so it's important to be able to objectively evaluate each. For instance, if you're highly skilled at sending clear messages, but you're lacking in the area of listening, your Social SPHERE is likely out of balance. In order to effectively communicate as your Best Self, you need to be able to do both well.

Refer back to your Social Skills Inventory and write down your scores here:

PART 1 (Sending Clear Messages) _____

Total Score: _____

PART 2 (Listening) _____

Total Score: _____

PART 3 (Giving and Receiving Feedback) _____

Total Score: _____

PART 4 (Handling Emotional Interactions) _____

Total Score: _____

If you scored between 1 and 21 in any of these areas, that is an indication that those areas require more attention from you. Keep those areas in mind as you progress through this chapter.

As for the "Who we socialize with" categories, I want you to think about how you might act differently within each of those groups. Sure, we all tend to be more relaxed and casual when we are around our family versus when we are with our work colleagues; that's a given. But we run into a problem when we are "faking it" in some of these circles. In other words, if your behavior around certain people is too far afield from who you really are, then you're not acting as your Best Self. For instance, when we say we agree with someone's viewpoint only because we don't want to be judged for holding an opposing belief, we are not being authentic. Or if we feel pressured to drink alcohol or do drugs with a certain crowd, when we usually would not, that's an example of not being our Best Self. If a coworker is gossiping or speaking poorly of a colleague, and we engage in that behavior even though it feels wrong, we aren't being our Best Self.

In order to help you discover whether you're showing up as the best version of yourself within all of your social circles, let's take this a step further by looking at a list of traits and choosing which ones apply to who you truly are within your Social SPHERE. When you are interacting with others—whether we're talking about a friend, family member, acquaintance, colleague, coworker, boss, employee, manager, teacher, vendor, assistant, waiter, flight attendant, or perfect stranger—what kind of person are you when you are being authentic?

As you look at the list of words, first circle the ones that jump out at you right away. Your eyes will likely land on those traits that ring true. Then, take a slower, more thoughtful look at the list and circle any other words that apply to you.

admirable	enthusiastic	leader	sensitive
affectionate	ethical	lively	sociable
agreeable	exciting	loving	sophisticated
altruistic	expert	magnanimous	spontaneous
amiable	fair	mature	steadfast
amicable	faithful	modest	stoic
appreciative	fearless	nurturing	suave
approachable	flexible	optimistic	subtle
at ease	forgiving	patient	supportive
attentive	forthright	perceptive	sweet
benevolent	friendly	personable	sympathetic
calm	functional	persuasive	teacherly
charming	fun-loving	philanthropic	tender
cheery	gallant	playful	thoughtful
compassionate	generous	polished	tolerant
conciliatory	gentle	popular	trusting
cool	genuine	principled	trustworthy
cooperative	giving	protective	unassuming
cordial	good-natured	rational	uncomplaining
courteous	gracious	reasonable	understanding
dedicated	grateful	relaxed	undogmatic
discreet	helpful	reliable	warm
dutiful	hospitable	respectful	watchful
dynamic	humorous	responsive	welcoming
eloquent	inspiring	romantic	
empathetic	intuitive	sage	
empowered	kind	selfless	

Anything about yourself that you find to be a positive attribute, and that you don't see above, write below:

_____   _____   _____

_____   _____   _____

_____   _____   _____

Are you starting to visualize, in an objective way, who you are within your Social SPHERE? Are you noticing any patterns? A good way to help you recognize these patterns in a more tangible way is to think about specific examples of these traits playing out in real life.

For example:

- If you selected "calm" from the list of positive traits, perhaps you chose to be calm when a waiter accidentally spilled something on your shirt, and it helped defuse an awkward situation.
- If you selected "teacherly" from the list of traits, maybe you took on a guiding role with a new employee who was struggling to understand a concept, and it made them feel safe and comfortable to ask questions.

Specific examples of my Best "Social" Self traits in action in my Social SPHERE are:

1. _____

2. _____

3. _____

I want you to paint a detailed mental picture of your Best "Social" Self, so let's keep going. The reason for going into such depth within this and all of your SPHERES is so that you can properly assess whether this particular SPHERE is one in which you need to spend a little extra time. In some seasons of our lives, we focus so wholly on one or two of our SPHERES that we easily lose touch with who we are within the others. It's all too easy to neglect some SPHERES altogether, and in fact, the Social SPHERE is often the first to fall by the wayside. In my own life, I have seen that when I don't have a structure that supports a social life, it creates challenges. If I decide to work in the evening, I have fewer opportunities to get dinner with friends. Maybe you've gotten into similar patterns. But as I discussed in *Best Self*, it's important to stay plugged in and authentic in your social life because maintaining a life beyond responsibility and embracing fun are deeply beneficial to your overall well-being. You can think of socializing as a form of exercise for your brain—it can help make you smarter in the same way that exercising your body makes you stronger. Remaining engaged in healthy socialization can also help ward off depression and improve our cognitive functioning.

Create Your Best "Social" Self

In the first chapter of *Best Self*, you took the time to create your own Best Self. Hopefully that exercise allowed you to more easily tap into the power of your authenticity, so that you can more often behave from that place. The more you are able to live as your Best Self, the more you will begin to see new opportunities and people reflecting back to you the positivity you are putting out into the world. Right now, I want you to do a similar exercise, but this time it will be through the lens of your social life. You will be creating your Best "Social" Self.

Recalling the list of traits you've already attributed to yourself within your Social SPHERE, consider the following questions.

1. Is your Best "Social" Self:

- a particular gender?
- an animal?
- a mystical creature? Or a wise voice inside yourself?
- a character inspired by a book or movie?

2. Does your Best "Social" Self behave in a particular way when someone is being:

- kind to you?
- threatening toward you?
- critical toward you?
- emotional with you?
- sarcastic with you?
- empathetic toward you?
- open with you?

3. Does your Best "Social" Self:

- send clear messages to others?
- listen attentively when others are sharing about themselves?

- give and receive feedback without judgment or condescension?
- handle emotional interactions well?

4. Does your Best "Social" Self move/dance/walk in a specific way?

5. Is your Best "Social" Self:

- the life of the party?
- the shoulder to cry on?
- the event planner?
- the talker?
- the listener?

6. What is your Best "Social" Self's superpower?

_____

_____

_____

_____

_____

_____

Write a full description of your Best "Social" Self here:

_____

_____

_____

_____

_____

_____

Now, how better to get a good visual of your Best "Social" Self than to draw it? You can use a pen, crayons, markers, colored pencils, whatever you like. Remember, we aren't all visual artists, so if it's not much more than a stick figure, that's okay! The image you have in your mind is likely more detailed than your drawing, and that mental picture is what's important. You can imagine the kind of looks I get when I sit down with major corporate executives to do this exercise! But the results are always worthwhile.

Draw your Best "Social" Self here:

Finally, take a moment to assign a name to your Best "Social" Self and write it at the top of the image you created.

Understand Your Anti "Social" Self

Create Your Anti "Social" Self

Now that you are on firm footing with who your Best "Social" Self is, let's turn our attention to your Anti "Social" Self (which doesn't necessarily translate to being "antisocial"!). Just as you defined and drew your Anti-Self when you read the book *Best Self*, you're going to do the same exercise but specifically within your Social SPHERE.

Below is a list of traits that could apply to how your Anti "Social" Self behaves. When you are not acting as your Best Self in a social setting, how do you tend to behave? I know this isn't the most positive thing to think about, but remember that things appear scarier in the dark, and we want to shed some light! Do not judge or condemn yourself while doing this exercise; instead, maintain an objective point of view, as if you were evaluating someone else. You will only stall your progress if you pass judgment on yourself. Instead, be honest about what can happen when you show up as your Anti-Self within your Social SPHERE so we can work toward eliminating that kind of behavior in the future. It takes a lot of courage to face the truth about how we sometimes behave, and it's really the first (and hardest) step toward reversing it. You're reading this book and doing this work so that you can improve your life all around, and it will be so worth it in the end.

As you peruse this list of traits, first circle the ones that jump out at you immediately, and then take a second pass and circle any additional ones that apply.

abrasive	critical	hostile	passive
abrupt	crude	impatient	perfectionist
angry	cynical	inconsiderate	perverse
anxious	deceitful	indiscreet	pessimistic
apathetic	demanding	inhibited	petty
argumentative	devious	insecure	pompous
arrogant	disagreeable	insincere	possessive
artificial	discouraging	insulting	resentful
awkward	dishonest	intolerant	rigid
bitter	disloyal	intoxicated	rude
boring	disrespectful	irritable	self-centered
brutal	disruptive	jealous	selfish
calculating	distractable	judgmental	stiff
callous	dogmatic	loud	stoic
cantankerous	domineering	malicious	tactless
charmless	dull	mannerless	tense
clingy	egotistical	mean	unappreciative
cold	fixed	moody	unfriendly
complaintive	follower	narcissistic	ungrateful
compulsive	gloomy	needy	unpleasant
conceited	greedy	negative	unpolished
conformist	gullible	obnoxious	unwelcoming
cowardly	hateful	overly opinionated	uptight
crass	haughty	paranoid	vain

Write any negative words you attribute to yourself within the context of your Social SPHERE here:

_____   _____   _____

_____   _____   _____

_____   _____   _____

Do you notice any patterns in the traits of your Anti "Social" Self? In other words, could you potentially group the characteristics you wrote down into specific categories? Maybe you tend to criticize others, or you become self-centered. Try to look at the traits objectively and see if you can identify larger patterns at play.

Patterns I notice in my Anti-Self traits as it relates to my Social SPHERE are:

_____

_____

_____

_____

BONUS EXERCISE:
SHARPEN YOUR LISTENING SKILLS

No matter how great we think we are at listening to others, we can always be better. The world is a loud place these days, with information coming at us from every possible angle 24/7, so it's a good idea to turn down the noise and hear what the people we care about are telling us.

For this exercise, gather together two to five friends, acquaintances, or family members. Each person in the group will take turns sitting in the "hot seat" and telling a story about him or herself. Afterward, the others are allowed to ask only follow-up questions. No one is allowed to offer advice, share their own stories, or change the subject. Once everyone has asked at least one clarifying question, thank the person in the hot seat for sharing their story, and move on to the next person.

This exercise will improve your listening skills, tap into your natural curiosity about other people's experiences, and connect you with your ability to pay closer attention. Additionally, as you each take your turn in the hot seat, you have the opportunity to feel heard and understood and to practice your communication skills. It's a win-win for everyone.

In the second chapter of the book, you imagined your Anti-Self. Now, I invite you to do that exercise again, but within the context of your Social SPHERE. When you are having an off day and you find yourself behaving as your Anti-Self, what does that look like? Again, it's important to identify that now to help you avoid those behaviors and actions later.

Recalling the list of traits you've already attributed to your Anti-Self within your Social SPHERE, consider the following questions.

1. Is your Anti "Social" Self:

- a particular gender?
- an animal?
- a mystical creature?
- a character inspired by a book or movie?

2. Does your Anti "Social" Self behave in a particular way when someone is being:

- kind to you?
- threatening toward you?
- critical of you?
- emotional with you?
- sarcastic with you?
- empathetic toward you?
- open with you?

3. Does your Anti "Social" Self move/dance/walk in a specific way?

4. Is your Anti "Social" Self:

- loud and obnoxious in a crowd?
- attention-seeking?
- a wallflower?
- afraid of socializing?
- a poor listener?
- overreactionary?

5. Does your Anti "Social" Self:

- struggle with sending clear messages to others?
- become inattentive or tune out when others are sharing about themselves?
- give abrasive or judgmental feedback?
- have an inability to gracefully receive constructive criticism from others?
- avoid emotional interactions or allow them to escalate unnecessarily?

Write a full description of your Anti "Social" Self here:

_____

_____

_____

Now, grab a pen or pencil, marker or paintbrush; it's time to sketch out your Anti "Social" Self. Get as detailed as you can!

Draw your Anti "Social" Self here:

Before you move on, assign a name to your Anti "Social" Self and write it at the top of the drawing.

Note: You might be thinking that you have more than one Anti "Social" Self, depending upon certain situations, triggers, interactions with specific people, etc. Try to draw the other versions of your Anti "Social" Self in a journal or on blank pieces of paper.

Next, write down three recent events or situations when you know your Anti "Social" Self had taken charge of a situation. Sometimes, we show different sides of ourselves based on who we are interacting with, so let's begin each of these scenarios by recalling who you were with and the details of your environment at the time.

Scenario 1:

• Who were you interacting with?

_____

_____

_____

• How, specifically, did you behave?

_____

_____

_____

• How did you feel following that behavior?

_____

_____

_____

Scenario 2:

• Who were you interacting with?

_____

_____

_____

• How, specifically, did you behave?

_____

_____

_____

- How did you feel following that behavior?

  _____

  _____

  _____

Scenario 3:

- Who were you interacting with?

  _____

  _____

  _____

- How, specifically, did you behave?

  _____

  _____

  _____

- How did you feel following that behavior?

_____

_____

_____

Next, ask yourself how you would handle those three situations if you were acting as your Best "Social" Self instead:

1. _____

2. _____

3. _____

Now that you have a very clear grasp on your Anti "Social" Self, the next time you're faced with a social situation that would usually bring him or her to the surface, you can actually choose to let your Best "Social" Self handle it instead. It can be a split-second decision—the moment you feel your Anti-Self wanting to react, you can opt for contrary action. Over time, as you make this conscious choice again and again, it will become automatic, and your Anti-Self will show up less and less. You will start to subconsciously summon your Best "Social" Self to rise to the occasion. In the meantime, start getting into the habit of taking a breath, clearing your mind, and being intentional about settling into your Best "Social" Self when you're in any given social situation.

You have the power to choose your behavior.

Based on your Social Skills Inventory scoring, the traits you identified earlier, and the three recent scenarios you just highlighted, what are some changes you can begin to make today in your Social SPHERE to help bolster your ability to show up as your Best "Social" Self?

For example:

- If you learned that you tend to avoid social settings altogether, and you often cancel plans last minute or sabotage your ability to attend upcoming social events, then you might make a deal with yourself to say "yes" to the next three invitations you receive and commit to following through on them.
- If you've realized that you often come across as self-centered when socializing and you focus only on yourself rather than talking and really listening to others, then you might write down that you're going to make a concerted effort to listen carefully and even quiz yourself later on three things you learned from others at a social event.

The point is, you want to define an *action* you can take in response to a negative pattern you've seen within your Social SPHERE.

Now, write down three behaviors you've noticed you need to improve and three corresponding actions you can take immediately to increase your odds of showing up as your Best Self in your Social SPHERE:

What I've Noticed: **Immediate Action I Can Take:**

1. _____   _____

2. _____   _____

3. _____   _____

Progress begins with taking an in-depth, honest look at yourself, and then creating an action-oriented plan for improving in areas that need it. Once you know what you need to do, it's vitally important to create some form of accountability. Referring back to the work you did in *Best Self* in creating a highly functional team of people around you, think about who on your team might keep you accountable for making the necessary changes in your Social SPHERE. If you don't currently have someone on your team who is appropriate for this task, think about someone you trust who might be willing. Write down your accountability partner here:

My accountability partner for my Social SPHERE is:

_____

Next, write down how you will ask them to help keep you on this new path. Will you ask them to help you say "yes" to social invitations for the next month? Will you ask them to check in with you weekly to be sure you've been behaving as your Best Self in social settings? Will you ask them to attend social gatherings with you and give you reminders when needed? Whatever your plan is, write it down here:

I will ask my accountability partner to help me by:

_____

_____

_____

_____

Tracking Your Progress

After a couple of weeks, return to this chapter and check in with yourself to see whether you've kept the forward momentum in your Social SPHERE. Do you feel you've made progress? Are there areas that require more of your attention? Write a few lines about how you've noticed yourself improving in your social life.

_____

_____

_____

_____

Be Your Best "Personal" Self

Your harshest critic lives between your two ears,
but you know what? Your best, most encouraging
friend can live between your two ears, too.
—*Best Self*

The single most important voice you hear is the voice inside your head. It is constant. Other than while asleep, that voice is ever present, and it says a lot of different things throughout the day. It's even speaking to you right now, in this very moment. Without question, that voice completely dictates both how you perceive the world and how you perceive yourself. What you say to yourself is more important than what anyone else says to you. The amazing news is that you can shift, sculpt, empower, and strengthen that voice. *That's* our goal in this chapter.

Let's begin by carefully considering your answers to these core questions:

1. What aspects of yourself do you genuinely love?

- It's often easier to think about those traits that we don't love, but I want you to set aside those thoughts and focus on what you truly love about yourself.

Write down what comes to mind here:

_____

_____

_____

_____

2. Do you put yourself first?

- Despite your long list of responsibilities, do you prioritize yourself and your needs above all else?
- If not, why not?
- If so, how are you currently putting yourself first?
- Are you compassionate toward yourself?

Write down your thoughts here:

_____

_____

_____

3. Do you make it a priority to properly manage stress in your life?

- Do you have a strategy for dealing with stress promptly, and in a healthy way?
- Do you find yourself feeling anxious, but aren't sure how to address it?
- Even when there are excessive demands on your time, do you still maintain proper hydration, sleep, exercise, nutrition, and meditation so that you are better able to meet those demands?

Write your thoughts and answers here:

_____

_____

_____

4. What messages do you say to yourself that are negative?

- Do you sometimes brow-beat yourself for your "failures"?
- Are there certain triggers that send your mind off into a tailspin of negative inner dialogue? If so, what are those triggers?
- What percentage of your daily inner dialogue is negative versus positive?

Write your thoughts and answers here:

_____

_____

_____

_____

5. What messages do you say to yourself that are positive?

- Do you celebrate your personal wins?
- Do you encourage yourself the way a coach would, by reminding yourself of your strength, and finding ways to improve upon areas that need it?
- Do you struggle to find your positive attributes in a specific area, such as your appearance, intelligence, competence, skills and abilities, or value?

Write your thoughts and answers here:

_____

_____

_____

After going through those questions, you might be feeling like you have more work to do in this Personal SPHERE than you thought. That's okay! This is a big area for all of us. From my experience working with clients, I can tell you that too often we don't focus on these topics until they have become a major problem. Why wait until then?

Because I want you to **be you, only better,** I want to help you strengthen the internal dialogue that is serving you and work to diminish the voices in your head that are lying to you. Your internal dialogue is filtering the world for you. What is the filter through which you're viewing the world and your daily experiences? Is that filter distorting your worldview in some way?

Here is the bottom line: any negative, critical messages you're sending to yourself are *not true*. You are doing the best you can, so why beat yourself up? Sure, there are people who lie, cheat, and steal—I'd just be very surprised if that's you. If it is, then that's most likely a past version of yourself, and you're now aware that it wasn't the right direction for your life. You owe it to yourself to keep your internal dialogue aligned with your Best Self.

Overview of Personal SPHERE

In *Best Self: Be You, Only Better*, the Personal SPHERE is divided into three sections:

- **Internal Dialogue**

  - What you're saying to yourself throughout the day. We send messages to ourselves about our intelligence, competence, skills and abilities, self-worth, value to others, and appearance.
  - There are patterns we can uncover about our internal dialogue, as well as an overall tone.
  - We all have a "locus of control." It is either:
    - *Internal*—meaning you believe you are in control of your life.
    - *External*—meaning you believe your life is dictated by outside forces or individuals.
    - *Chance*—meaning you believe it's the luck of the draw as to whether you have a good day or bad day.
  - Exercises that help you identify your internal dialogue start on page 133 of *Best Self: Be You, Only Better*.

- **Self-care**

  - How compassionate you are toward yourself.
  - This includes proper stress management.

- There's a Stress Quiz starting on page 140 of *Best Self*, and it will help you discern how good you are at managing stress as it comes in.
- Practical methods for self-care are:
  - Mindful breathing
  - Physical exercise
  - Celebrating your life
  - Maintaining proper sleep hygiene
  - Unplugging from tech
  - Connecting with your relaxation/guided visualization

- **Passions**

  - Those activities that make you feel as though you are "in the flow of life" and vibrating at your highest frequency.
  - Stepping out of your everyday routine to do something that both excites you and connects you with your purpose for living.

As you can see, the Personal SPHERE is all about how well you are caring for yourself, and how connected you are to your life. The idea in this workbook chapter is to uncover or rediscover truths about yourself, to cut the "fat" in your thinking patterns and your inner conversations so that you can function at a higher and more abundant level, to allow yourself to have a voice, to find out what it really means to respect yourself, and to realize your gifts and put them to work in your life.

Creating Your Best Self Mindscape

Let's set the stage for the work you're going to be doing here, and for significantly improving your Personal SPHERE. First, take a look at page 133 in *Best Self: Be You, Only Better* and review your responses to the Internal Dialogue exercises starting on that page.

Since you completed those answers, has your internal dialogue changed at all? Write down an overview of the inner conversations you've been having with yourself lately.

_____

_____

_____

That constant dialogue you have with yourself all day long actually creates an internal landscape—for the sake of this conversation, let's refer to it as your mindscape. Imagine if someone were to enter into your current mindscape—what would they see? Is it a harsh environment, like the surface of a planet riddled with explosive volcanoes and hot, dry air, with nowhere to escape? Or would they step into a lush, welcoming place, with gentle ocean breezes and a hammock strung between two palm trees? If you're always beating yourself up, obsessing about something you did or said, blaming others for your feelings, focusing on something you're ashamed of, or thinking toxic thoughts about others in your circles, then your mindscape isn't a pleasant place to exist.

Alternatively, if you're telling yourself that you are capable, kind, and confident, then your mindscape is a softer, gentler, *safe* place. An imperative aspect of your mindscape is gratitude. By making a concerted effort to reassure yourself with a grateful spirit, your mindscape becomes a space that lifts you up rather than drags you down.

Right now, I want you to get really specific about your mindscape. What does it look like? How does it make you feel? What kind of thoughts does it tend to create? Write your answers here:

I'd describe my current mindscape as:

_____

_____

_____

My mindscape makes me feel:

_____

_____

_____

The kinds of thoughts my mindscape generates are:

_____

_____

_____

Now, ask yourself this question: Does your mindscape accurately reflect and support you in being your Best Self? Or could it use a little renovation? The goal here is to greet each day by turning inward and ensuring that you are creating a peaceful mindscape in which your thoughts can generate all day long—a place from which it's easy to think and behave as your Best Self out in the world.

By intentionally creating this mental imagery, you can now choose to go into this headspace and remain there, no matter what challenges the day throws at you. When you do this, your inner dialogue can naturally shift toward the positive. Your internal landscape reflects your external experience. By being in this space, you're more likely to see the good in any situation, to remain calm when outside stressors occur, and to approach yourself and others with a spirit of acceptance instead of defensiveness or frustration.

The Outside Noise Quiz

In *Best Self*, as summarized at the start of this chapter, one of the topics in the Personal SPHERE is your locus of control. I wanted to spend a little extra time on that subject here in the workbook, because I think it's an incredibly valuable tool. Another way to think about your locus of control is to consider whether you tend to assign blame for your circumstances in the external world, or to take responsibility for your life.

When someone says something negative about you, that's outside noise. World news is outside noise. Gossip is outside noise. Someone else's negative opinion of how you live your life is outside noise. You get the point. The question is—do you choose to engage in that outside noise, and to allow it to affect your internal peace? Does outside noise dictate how you feel about yourself, or about your place in the world? Let's investigate a bit with this quiz.

1. If you have an issue with someone at work, do you tend to blame the other person? Do you often find yourself saying or thinking, "If I just had a different manager (team, assistant, etc.), I would love my job"?

   ○ YES   ○ NO

2. When you're driving and someone cuts you off, do you often get upset, or even yell or flip them off? Do you feel violated by their behavior, and like they should "learn how to drive"?

   ○ YES   ○ NO

3. If you're having a disagreement with your intimate partner, do you often leave the conversation or argument thinking to yourself that he or she is the problem in the relationship, and if they "would

only change" in some way or another, then you'd get along just fine?

○ **YES**   ○ **NO**

4. Do you chalk up your troubles to "bad luck" in some (or every) area of your life, and believe that's why you struggle with certain things?

○ **YES**   ○ **NO**

5. If you're suffering to any degree in any part of your life, are you pretty easily able to pin it on another person, place, or thing?

○ **YES**   ○ **NO**

If some, or any, of those statements even slightly fit your current thinking, then it's likely that you tend to allow outside noise to affect your internal peace. This is the same thing as having an "external locus of control." The trouble with this mentality is that it causes you to give all of your power away.

The goal is to have less noise and more harmony. The way you have more harmony is by letting the good in and cutting back on the noise. If, instead, you're playing the blame game and adopting a victim mentality, then you're giving in to the noise and standing in your own way of improving your life.

If your level of enjoyment at your job is dictated by your manager's mood, then you are powerless to change it. You can only control yourself; you can't control anyone else. Going through life letting the outside noise define how you feel, think, and behave is like being emotionally handcuffed.

I want you to begin to shift your thinking across the board and to shut off that outside noise. Sure, it's always going to be there. But you do not have to allow it in. Your life is your own. You choose your emotions. You choose your reactions. You choose your behavior. Your personal life will change in incredibly powerful ways when you embrace an internal locus of control that allows you to take back the reins.

If your boss is tough on you, take the feedback and adapt your behavior at work, but don't allow that person's opinion to change the story you're telling yourself about your abilities.

Someone else is a poor driver—well, you maintain safe control of your car and you move away from that person. Focus on you, not on them.

Your partner disagrees with you on something—they are their own person and they are allowed to have their viewpoints. Respectfully and lovingly agree to disagree, and work toward a compromise. Don't allow it to change your entire opinion of them or of the relationship.

Certainly there are times when forces outside of our control come into play, but you have the ability to adapt, to evolve, and to face each challenge head-on. Don't just give up and decide you're cursed with bad luck.

If you're suffering, it's not anyone else's responsibility to address it for you. That power rests in your hands. If something isn't working, change it.

As you continue the work in this and future chapters, come back to this quiz and check in with yourself to make sure you are maintaining an internal locus of control, and not allowing all that outside noise to shape your beliefs about yourself.

Your Current Personal Life versus
Your Best Self Personal Life

Now let's spend some time looking at the current state of your personal life (your internal dialogue, attention to self-care, etc.). From the lists of traits below, write down ones that apply to how you're currently thinking and behaving within your Personal SPHERE.

abundant	dedicated	fun-loving	magnanimous
accepting	diligent	fulfilled	mature
accountable	discreet	functional	modest
affectionate	dutiful	generous	nurturing
agreeable	dynamic	gentle	optimistic
amicable	easygoing	genuine	patient
appreciative	empathetic	giving	peaceful
at ease	empowered	good-natured	perceptive
attentive	enthusiastic	gracious	persuasive
benevolent	ethical	grateful	playful
bountiful	exciting	helpful	prayerful
calm	expert	hospitable	principled
celebratory	fair	humorous	prioritizing of self
cheerful	faithful	inspiring	proactive
cheering on	fearless	intuitive	protective
compassionate	flexible	kind	rational
complimentary	forgiving	leader	reasonable
conciliatory	forthright	lively	relaxed
cool	friendly	loving	reliable

respectful	sensitive	teacherly	understanding
responsive	sincere	tender	undogmatic
romantic	spiritual	thoughtful	warm
sage	stable	tolerant	welcoming
secure	steadfast	trusting	wise
self-aware	supportive	trustworthy	
self-reliant	sweet	unassuming	
self-sufficient	sympathetic	uncomplaining	

abrasive	crude	hostile	perfectionist
abusive	cruel	immature	perverse
angry	cynical	impatient	pessimistic
annoying	damaging	inane	petty
anxious	dark	inconsiderate	poisonous
apathetic	deceitful	inhibited	pompous
argumentative	delusional	insecure	quitter
arrogant	demanding	insincere	resentful
artificial	denial	insulting	rigid
barbed	disagreeable	intolerant	rude
bitter	discouraging	irritable	ruthless
brutal	dishonest	jealous	scary
calculating	disloyal	judgmental	self-obsessed
callous	disrespectful	lame	severe
cantankerous	dogmatic	malicious	tense
coarse	domineering	mean	threatening
cold	egotistical	menacing	unappreciative
cold-hearted	failure	moody	unfriendly
complaintive	follower	narcissistic	ungrateful
compulsive	gloomy	nasty	unpleasant
conceited	grim	negative	unpolished
conformist	gullible	obnoxious	unwelcoming
cowardly	hateful	offensive	uptight
critical	haughty	paranoid	vain

How I am currently within my personal life:

_____   _____   _____

_____   _____   _____

_____   _____   _____

_____   _____   _____

Take a look at the traits you wrote down, and let's consider any negative traits on your list. How are those playing out in your personal life? Has your Anti-Self been known to overshadow your Best Self at times and tell you lies about who you are, what you're capable of, and what you deserve? Have you ever found yourself indulging in a blame game, beating yourself up, or neglecting yourself in some way? We've all been there, and the first step toward breaking patterns like that is to acknowledge them. And the best way to acknowledge them is to find specific examples of them in your life.

For the first question in each scenario, think about what was going on in your world at the time. Were you preparing for a presentation at work? Were you disciplining your child when he or she was misbehaving? Were you interacting with your partner or another family member? Were you juggling an endless to-do list, burning the candle at both ends and trying to be everything to everyone? Think about the external trigger or scenario that was playing out.

Scenario 1:

• What was going on externally?

_____

_____

_____

• What was your internal dialogue telling you?

_____

_____

_____

• How did you feel during this situation?

_____

_____

_____

- What were the outcomes or consequences of this scenario?

_____

_____

_____

Scenario 2:

- What was going on externally?

_____

_____

_____

- What was your internal dialogue telling you?

_____

_____

_____

- How did you feel during this situation?

_____

_____

_____

- What were the outcomes or consequences of this scenario?

_____

_____

_____

Scenario 3:

- What was going on externally?

_____

_____

_____

- What was your internal dialogue telling you?

_____

_____

_____

- How did you feel during this situation?

_____

_____

_____

- What were the outcomes or consequences of this scenario?

_____

_____

_____

We will come back to this exercise in a moment, to see how your Best Self would have handled each scenario. But first, look back at the same list of traits, and identify ones that accurately describe how you are in terms of your relationship with yourself (inner dialogue, self-care, stress management, etc.) when you are being your **Best Self**.

For example, when you're firmly rooted within your Best Self, perhaps you express gratitude on a regular basis, so you might write down "grateful." Or you might be more "nurturing" toward yourself, or "compassionate."

How I am when I'm being my Best Self in my personal life:

_____   _____   _____

_____   _____   _____

_____   _____   _____

_____   _____   _____

Now, I want you to think about some specific examples of the Best Self personal traits you selected as they play out in real life.

- For example, if you selected "patient" from the list of positive traits, perhaps you can think of a time when you made a mistake of some kind, but instead of berating yourself, you chose to be patient and give yourself space to make an error and learn from it.

- Or if you selected "complimentary" from the list of traits, an example might be when you caught a glimpse of yourself in the mirror and thought, "Hey, I'm looking good!"

Specific examples of how I behave in my Personal SPHERE when I'm being my Best Self are:

1. _____

2. _____

3. _____

4. _____

1. Can you see a difference between how you're currently operating within your personal life versus how you operate when you are being your Best Self?

    ○ **YES**   ○ **NO**

2. If yes, then in what area(s) do you see a difference? Explain:

Internal Dialogue: _____

_____

_____

(Example: Currently, when I talk to myself about my skills and abilities, I am very critical. I tell myself that I'll never measure up and that I'll never get anywhere in my job or relationships. But as my Best Self, I am forgiving of myself, am accepting of my flaws, and reassure myself that I am capable of growth.)

Self-care: _____

_____

_____

(Example: Currently, I rarely make it a point to think about how I'm dealing with stress. Instead, I get overcome with anxiety to the point of barely being able to function. But when I'm being my Best Self, I create time to meditate and visualize positive outcomes.)

Passions: _____

_____

_____

(Example: Currently, I do not feel connected to my passions, and I do not take the time to explore them or put them into practice. However, when I'm being my Best Self, I prioritize my passions and find the time to do activities that reflect them.)

3. Now, look back at the three scenarios you wrote earlier. If you'd been acting as your Best Self, what would have been different?

Scenario 1:

- What was going on externally?

_____

_____

_____

- If you'd been acting as your Best Self, what would your internal dialogue have been?

_____

_____

_____

- How would you have felt if your Best Self had been in control?

_____

_____

_____

- What would the outcomes have been?

_____

_____

_____

Scenario 2:

- What was going on externally?

_____

_____

_____

- If you'd been acting as your Best Self, what would your internal dialogue have been?

_____

_____

_____

• How would you have felt if your Best Self had been in control?

_____

_____

_____

• What would the outcomes have been?

_____

_____

_____

Scenario 3:

• What was going on externally?

_____

_____

_____

- If you'd been acting as your Best Self, what would your internal dialogue have been?

_____

_____

_____

- How would you have felt if your Best Self had been in control?

_____

_____

_____

- What would the outcomes have been?

_____

_____

_____

Creating an Action Plan

Are you starting to see the ways that your Best Self can help you produce better outcomes in your personal life? I know it can be challenging to focus on our Personal SPHERE (until there's a problem, and I don't want you to wait that long!), but in order to show up as your Best Self as a parent, a role model, an employee or supervisor, a friend, a son, a daughter, a sibling, and so on, you *must* show up for yourself first.

So, what are some changes you can begin to make today in your Personal SPHERE to help bolster your ability to show up as your Best "Personal" Self?

For example:

- I've noticed that I have a strong tendency to judge myself as incapable of taking on new challenges, so I'm going to create a mantra that specifically states how adaptable I am, and how I'm able to confidently undertake new tasks.
- I often put myself at the end of the list, and by the time I get there, I'm too tired to take care of myself properly. So, the action I'm going to take is to prioritize myself each and every day, and take time for me before I begin taking care of others in my life.

The idea is to define *action* you can take in response to a negative pattern you've seen developing within your Personal SPHERE.

Now write down three areas you've noticed you need to improve and three corresponding changes you can make immediately to increase your odds of showing up as your Best Self in your Personal SPHERE:

What I've Noticed: **Immediate Action I Can Take:**

1. _____   _____

2. _____   _____

3. _____   _____

Think about the team of people around you, and who might be the right fit for keeping you accountable to making the necessary changes in your Personal SPHERE. If you don't currently have someone on your team who is appropriate for this task, think about someone you trust who might be willing. Write down your accountability partner here:

My accountability partner for my Personal SPHERE is:

_____

Next, write down how you will ask them to help keep you on this new path.

- Will you ask them to remind you to not judge yourself so harshly the next time you talk negatively about yourself?
- Will you ask them to remind you each day to check in with yourself on your internal dialogue?
- Will you plan some "self-care" activities together, such as a meditation class or just a quiet stroll around a park?

Whatever your accountability ideas are, write them down here:

I will ask my accountability partner to help me by:

_____

_____

_____

_____

Tracking Your Progress

After a couple of weeks, return to this chapter and check in with yourself to see whether you've kept the forward momentum in your Personal SPHERE. Do you feel you've made progress? Are there areas that require more of your attention? Write a few lines about how you've noticed yourself improving in your personal life.

_____

_____

_____

_____

_____

_____

Be Your Best "Health" Self

When our physical health is operating at its
highest level, the possibilities for what we can
accomplish in this world are endless.
—*Best Self*

What does better health mean to you? We're always aging, always evolving, and our bodies are always going through some process, but for you specifically, what does better health really look like? That's what I want you to focus on as you read this chapter. This isn't about achieving someone else's idea of good health, or measuring up to your social media feeds' definition of healthy. This is about your own specific, unique journey toward better health. Once you are able to articulate what that is, then you're much more likely to be able to achieve your health goals. Here are some questions to get you thinking about your health.

1. ENERGY: Do you have enough energy to get through your day?

    • Do you lack the energy needed to do activities you love, such as
      playing with your kids, running with your dog, taking hikes in
      nature?
    • Do you have health challenges, such as respiratory issues, heart
      problems, autoimmune disorders, etc., that interfere with daily
      life?

    Write down your thoughts and answers:

    _____

    _____

    _____

    _____

2. PREVENTION: Do you feel you could be doing more in the area
    of prevention, so that your health is more protected now and in
    the future?

    • Are there areas such as nutrition and exercise where you know
      you have room for improvement, but you just haven't made the
      effort to program your lifestyle in such a way to preserve your
      health?

Write down your thoughts and answers:

_____

_____

_____

3. POWER: Do you feel you have power over your health?

- Do you make decisions on a daily basis that have a positive impact on your overall health, or does that feel like a constant struggle?
- Does your Best Self look out for your health, acknowledge when something feels "off," and address it right away? Or do you often sweep potential health issues under the rug and hope they'll resolve themselves?

Write down your thoughts and answers:

_____

_____

_____

Your health isn't something you can put on "hold" and come back to when you aren't as busy. Your body works hard for you so that you can go out and do all the things you want and need to. Keeping your physical health in check is foundational, so your job is to discover how you can properly maintain it while living your life.

Lately, I've spent a lot of time working on stretching. I know that might sound funny, but I've discovered that keeping limber is incredibly important. Before, when I'd bend to touch my toes, my joints would creak so much that it sounded like a haunted mansion! But I'm six foot five, I travel a *lot*, and I sit a lot to work and write. As a result, my muscles and ligaments had become super tight. That may not sound like a big deal, but it can have detrimental effects on the body. I'm really glad I came to this realization and started incorporating more yoga and stretching into my routine. It's made a huge difference.

What's a simple thing you could start doing that would make a huge difference in your own health journey? Do you want to lose weight? Do you wish you could have less pain, more energy, increased stamina, better quality sleep, more consistent exercise, better blood work results, etc.? There are small, achievable steps you can start taking right away that can start you on your path toward any of those goals. Rather than getting overwhelmed by focusing on the end result you desire, the idea is to start today with adjustments to your lifestyle that will pay off in the long run.

We also want to take time in this chapter to acknowledge what is great about your health today! That means different things to different people. Perhaps you've already come a long way in some area of your health—in which case, you need to celebrate that win. Or maybe you've always had excellent blood work. For me, good health means I am physically able to exercise and get a lot of things accomplished in my day-to-day life without being held back. And staying in good health means that I work up a sweat once a day, no matter what. For you, good health could mean morning walks, golfing, doing yoga, hiking, riding a bike, meal-prepping for the week ahead, taking certain supplements you've found to be effective, and so on. Let's discover what good health really means to you and come up with a plan for achieving, maintaining, and preserving it.

YOUR HEALTH IN YOUR HANDS

Scientists have discovered so much about the role genetics play in our overall health and risk factors for certain diseases, and they still have much to learn. But perhaps the most exciting thing to come from all the gene sequencing and research is this: you are, by no means, "doomed" to get a certain illness because of your genes. In fact, your genes account for only a small percentage of your health risk factors—the truth is, your environment plays a much larger role. And your environment also refers to your behaviors. While you can't control your DNA, you can absolutely control your behaviors. So grab hold of this opportunity to really dissect your relationship with your physical health, and begin to direct it in a purposeful way. Your health, right now and in your future, rests in your hands.

Rate Your Health

Look back at the Health Inventory you completed on *Best Self* page 180, where you rated your health on a scale of 1–10. A 1 means you recognize that your Health SPHERE needs your immediate attention because you are facing health challenges, and a 10 means you are already taking excellent care of your overall health and have little to no room for improvement in this area.

Transfer your previous answer here:

My past physical health rating was _____ as of _____ (date)

Now, I'd like you to rate your current state of health. As we know, health is not static—it is always changing and evolving with time.

My *current* physical health rating is _____ as of _____ (date)

Note: If your rating is between 1 and 5, that is an indication that your physical health requires much more attention from you. If you rated between 6 and 10, that means you are already making effort to take care of your overall health, but your Best Self may not always be leading the charge in this SPHERE. I can tell you right now—if you rated your physical health as a 10, then you are the Michael Jordan of health. You're a star, an anomaly. I personally believe we all have room for improvement. Maybe you disagree, but I'd still encourage you to read on and engage in the rest of this chapter.

Has your health rating changed over time? If so, write down why you believe it has. For instance, have you begun exercising more regularly, or have you gone on a specific diet? Alternatively, have you been under a lot of stress that's having a negative impact on your health? Or have you been diagnosed with something that you're still learning how to manage?

My physical health rating has changed over time because:

_____

_____

_____

Next, let's celebrate some of your health "wins." These are behaviors that are working for you and that you plan to continue. Some examples are:

- I regularly exercise in a way that feels good for my body and doesn't cause injury.
- I eat foods that I know are supporting and preserving my physical health, rather than foods that have a negative impact on my health.
- I regularly go in for checkups with a physician or specialist that I trust.

The following are behaviors that are working to protect, promote, and preserve my health, and the ways in which they are doing so:

- _____ How: _____

- _____ How: _____

- _____ How: _____

As you work through the rest of this chapter, think about areas that you can start improving upon, and behaviors you can begin to adopt in order to further strengthen and preserve your health going forward.

Current Picture of Your Health SPHERE

The lists of words below are some common traits when it comes to the way we approach our overall health. Of course, we all have good days and bad days, but think about traits that accurately describe your own attitude and resulting behaviors in general. If you feel "energetic" 8 out of 10 days, then it's safe to describe yourself as energetic, for example.

Closely look at these lists of traits and then write down ones that generally apply to you. Feel free to write in any words you don't see listed here, too.

accepting	electric	intuitive	relaxed
active	empowered	mindful	reliable
adaptable	enduring	moderate	resilient
alive	energetic	motivated	resolute
at ease	enthusiastic	muscular	restful
athletic	exerciser	nourished	satiated
attentive	exerting	nutritious	satisfied
awake	fit	organized	savoring
aware	flexible	peaceful	self-controlled
balanced	flourishing	positive	self-restrained
better	fresh	powerful	self-willed
body-positive	glowing	practicing	spontaneous
bright	goal-oriented	prepared	sporty
brisk	good habits	preventative	steadfast
busy	grateful	prioritizing	strong
calm	happy	proactive	sustainable
clean	health-conscious	pure	tough
committed	healthful	purposeful	undogmatic
content	healthy	rational	unyielding
curious	hearty	reasonable	vibrant
dedicated	hydrated	recreational	vigorous
determined	hygienic	refreshed	well
disciplined	informed	regimented	zestful
driven	in-shape	regular	
dynamic	interested	rejuvenated	

---

absentminded	depleted	dragging	gloomy
addicted	depressed	drowsy	gluttonous
ailing	discontented	dull	gym rat
anxious	discouraging	empty	"hangry"
apathetic	diseased	exhausted	harping on self
avoidant	dispirited	failing	idle
careless	dissatisfied	famished	ignorant
craving	distracted	feeble	ill
dehydrated	distressed	forgetful	inactive
denying	dogmatic	frail	inattentive

indifferent	moody	rash	sweet tooth
indulgent	negative	reckless	tense
injured	negligent	resigning	tired
in pain	nervous	resistant	unaware
insatiable	noncommittal	restless	undernourished
intoxicated	oblivious	run-down	underweight
irregular	obsessed	sad	unhappy
jealous	over-eater	sickly	unhealthy
jittery	overindulgent	sleep-deprived	unmindful
judgmental	overweight	sloppy	unmotivated
lazy	passable	slow	unprepared
lethargic	pessimistic	sluggish	uptight
lifeless	queasy	starved	weak
miserable	quitting	stressed	worn out

How I am currently within my Health SPHERE:

_____   _____   _____

_____   _____   _____

_____   _____   _____

_____   _____   _____

Now, let's identify any problem areas you are having in the management of your Health SPHERE by looking at some recent scenarios that show the choices you've made that affected your health in a less than ideal way.

Scenario 1:

- What were the specific circumstances?

  _____

  _____

  _____

  (Example: I had been sick for a week and the symptoms were only getting worse.)

- How, specifically, did you behave?

  _____

  _____

  _____

  (Example: I kept on with my busy schedule and never went to the doctor. I took medications to mask the symptoms, but didn't try to figure out the cause.)

- What was the result of that behavior?

  _____

  _____

  _____

(Example: I got a fever and almost passed out while driving. I had to go to urgent care, where I learned I had strep throat and needed antibiotics. I ended up missing several days of work, but if I'd gone to the doctor earlier, I would've missed much less.)

Scenario 2:

• What were the specific circumstances?

_____

_____

_____

• How, specifically, did you behave?

_____

_____

_____

• What was the result of that behavior?

_____

_____

_____

Scenario 3:

- What were the specific circumstances?

_____

_____

_____

- How, specifically, did you behave?

_____

_____

_____

- What was the result of that behavior?

_____

_____

_____

Next, ask yourself how you would handle those three scenarios if you were acting as your Best "Health" Self instead:

1. _____

2. _____

3. _____

The next time you are faced with any kind of circumstance that involves your health, stop and think before you act. Ask yourself, "How would my Best Self handle this situation?" It only takes a moment's awareness to make a decision that is in your best interest, rather than one that can hurt your health.

The Best Self Version of Your Health

Now, take another look at that same list of words, and think about which ones apply to you when your Best Self is running the show in your Health SPHERE. Think about those days when you are caring for your body, eating foods that nourish you properly, exercising in a way that feels good, and giving yourself credit for the work you're doing.

How I am when my Best Self
is in charge of my Health SPHERE:

_____   _____   _____

_____   _____   _____

_____   _____   _____

It could be that there's overlap between your current list and your Best Self list. Or there might be a significant difference between them. Now that you've seen them side by side, you can gauge for yourself how far off you are from your Best Self being in charge of your health.

Now, I want you to think about some specific examples of the Best Self health traits you selected as they play out in real life.

For example:

- If you selected "informed" from the list of positive traits, perhaps an example is that you often read up on the latest health trends or listen to health-oriented podcasts and apply what you learn to your own life.
- If you selected "preventative" from the list of traits, maybe an example is that you know your family is prone to heart conditions, so you take extra precautions to maintain a healthy heart through diet, cardiovascular exercise at the gym, and your doctor's other recommendations.

Specific examples of my Best "Health" Self traits in action are:

1. _____

2. _____

3. _____

Refer to these examples any time you need a reminder of how your Best Self can look out for your health. You can always choose behaviors that prioritize your physical well-being.

Habit Shifts

So much of your physical health is related to your habits—both good and bad. You can think of habits as computer programs that are just running in the background. You're not actively using the program, but it's there, running its processes and taking up space on your hard drive. There's great power in habits, though, because you can harness them and direct them to do good for you.

Let's take a look at some of the most common habits that have an impact on your health and see if there are some simple shifts or adjustments you can make so your habits better support your health. The fewer decisions you have to make around your health activities on a daily basis, the easier keeping them a priority becomes.

Do you have any habits that you know have a negative impact on your health? (That is, smoking, vaping, taking illicit drugs, abusing prescription drugs, drinking alcohol in excess, consuming a lot of processed or fast food and soda, etc.)

My current habits that could have a negative impact on my health:

1. _____

2. _____

3. _____

4. _____

5. _____

Now, look at each habit on your list. Rather than thinking about trying to get rid of one or all of them (since we don't really get rid of habits; we *replace* them), think about how you could adjust the habit or replace it with something that will help you with your health goals.

For instance, if you have a habit of drinking a caffeinated drink of some kind in the afternoon for a burst of energy, think of replacing that drink with a nutrient-dense snack such as an apple and almond butter.

Possible replacements that will have a positive impact on my health:

1. _____

2. _____

3. _____

4. _____

5. _____

I want you to see that your habits are not at all permanent. Give yourself a good two to three weeks to really establish your new health habits, as it takes about that length of time for your brain to click into autopilot. Yes, it might seem foreign at first when you replace a harmful habit with a helpful one, but stick with it and you'll be surprised when, one day, you automatically do the new habit without even having to think about it. This is how people who exercise every day get to that point—they just keep doing it until their body understands the routine. Then, they don't even have to think about it anymore! It just seems to happen. This reflex can happen for you, too. It's like brushing your teeth.

BEHAVIOR = RESULT

For an entire week, log anything and everything you do that relates to your health: what you eat, when you exercise, your mood, how you sleep, etc. At the end of the week, see if you notice connections between your diet, activities, energy, etc. Maybe you went out to eat with coworkers for lunch at a fast-food restaurant, then spent the rest of the afternoon feeling tired and irritable. You might draw a conclusion that it's in your best interest to avoid burgers, french fries, and soda on busy workdays because they deplete your energy. Perhaps you woke up early one morning to do twenty minutes of stretching and felt noticeably less pain in your neck and back as you went about your day.

Then, spend the next week adjusting your habits based on what you learned from this data collection exercise. This is a simple way to bring more awareness to your health and wellness, and how your behavior affects how you feel. The idea here is to begin to identify cause and effect, behavior and result.

Continue, Stop, Start

Now, let's look at the entire picture of your Health SPHERE and consider the areas in which you're already thriving, areas in which you're potentially sabotaging your health, and areas in which you need to add in some new behavior(s) in order to bolster your health. This is a "continue, stop, start" exercise, designed to help you clarify how your behaviors need to change in order to meet your health goals. Fill out each of these sections:

I need to continue:

_____   _____

_____   _____

_____   _____

I need to stop:

_____   _____

_____   _____

I need to start:

_____   _____

_____   _____

Isn't it nice to have a very clear list of what you need to do? This is the first and most difficult step toward achieving your optimal health. So many people live their whole lives stuck in a state of "I wish I felt better," or "I wish I had more energy," or "If only I wasn't sick all the time." But now you have a clear action plan, a path forward so that you don't have to "wish" and "hope" anymore. You can behave your way to success.

Your Health Accountability Partner(s)

Research indicates that having an accountability partner, someone who is committed to helping you attain your goals, exponentially increases your odds of success, especially in the area of health. Who is someone in your life who would, for example, go on walks with you in the morning, or have healthy lunches with you in the afternoon? Or someone who is willing to text or email you daily with motivational reminders to stay on track, and to congratulate you on meeting your goals along the way? Think about a person, or several people, who will help you stay on this new, healthy path.

My accountability partner(s) for my Health SPHERE is/are:

Next, write down how you will ask them to help you stay account-able to your health goals.

I will ask my accountability partner(s) to help me by:

_____

_____

_____

Tracking Your Progress

After a couple of weeks, return to this chapter and check in with your-self to see whether you've kept the forward momentum in your Health SPHERE. Have you made some headway? Are there any areas that require more of your attention? Write a few lines about how you've noticed yourself improving in your health life.

_____

_____

_____

Be Your Best "Education" Self

Even if you never liked school, if you believe you have a learning
difference or you think you just don't like the process of taking
in new information, your Best Self is thirsty for knowledge—your
job is simply to figure out what interests you on a deep level.

—*Best Self*

When I was writing *Best Self* and thinking about the Educational SPHERE, I seriously considered naming it the Evolution SPHERE. I believe that we are always, always evolving—we are taking in information from our experiences and making subtle adjustments to the way we live accordingly. But this shouldn't be a passive evolutionary process. I believe we can evolve with purpose and intention—the key is to stay in learning mode. Educating ourselves, stretching our minds and imaginations, and learning about subjects that interest us is one way that we can improve upon our Best Self and truly create our best life. We also have to stretch ourselves past what we believe to be our ability; that's how we create growth in our lives.

Before you dive into the work in this chapter, consider these core questions.

1. EXTINGUISH: Are you willing to acknowledge and then remove any biases or limiting beliefs around your ability to learn and evolve?

- Did you struggle in school, or in a particular subject, and you've been telling yourself a story about your inability to learn as a result?
- Have you often felt like you're just too old to learn new information, or that there's just no more "room" in your brain?

Write your thoughts and answers here:

_____

_____

_____

_____

2. EXPAND: Are you routinely pushing yourself outside of your comfort zone to try new things, and are you stretching yourself to acquire new skills and knowledge?

- Do you consider yourself a "sponge," always soaking up new information?
- Do you enjoy reading, listening to audiobooks or podcasts, or even taking "master classes" online?
- Do you often select "infotainment" style television programming, in which you're learning something new while also being entertained?
- Do you take an interest in learning more about yourself, what makes you tick, why you behave in certain ways, etc.? (Since you're doing this workbook, I'd guess the answer to this one is a resounding "yes!")

Write your thoughts and answers here:

_____

_____

_____

_____

_____

3. EXPLORE: Do you seek to understand how others experience and view the world, especially people who are different from you in some way?

- Have you sought out people who come from a different background, or who are from another part of the world, and asked them about their experience?
- Have you traveled to other regions in order to experience, firsthand, another culture?

Write your thoughts and answers here:

_____

_____

_____

_____

_____

4. EXPRESS: Do you find ways to express, teach, or share your interests and passions?

- Do you get excited about something you've learned and then share it with people in your life?
- Do you seek out other people who share your interests?

Write your thoughts and answers here:

_____

_____

_____

_____

_____

As I write these words, it's been about eighteen months since I embarked upon my journey toward becoming an author. I've learned a lot since starting down this path, and I learn more each day. I'm always looking for ways to push myself and imagine fresh and innovative ways to help people. There's so much fascinating research out there, so many powerful techniques, and I love learning about them and then putting my own twist on them. I enjoy adding more tools to my tool kit all the time.

I wouldn't have been able to predict a year and a half ago that I'd be doing what I'm doing now. It's true that we can't know exactly the ways in which we are going to evolve, but it's always incredibly rewarding to look back and see how far we've come. I've seen the powerful results and rewards that come from expecting more of myself and stepping way out of my comfort zone. It's hard at first, but it gets easier the more you do it!

We have to constantly break our own rules, because those rules can hold us back from our potential. Yes, stretching is painful; it's challenging. It requires a lot of blind faith. Complacency is the enemy of evolution. That's exactly why we see so many people in jobs that feel empty—like they're just clocking in and out, doing the same thing again and again. That's what happens when we don't push ourselves. Your Best Self wants so much more for you than that.

In this chapter, my aim is to inspire you to tap into your passions and challenge yourself to get deeply curious and learn more than you ever thought possible. I also want to help you embrace failure as the ultimate learning experience and a wonderful indication that you are taking risks, putting yourself out there, and being curious.

Uncovering Your Innate Curiosity

When thinking about your Educational SPHERE, rather than focusing solely on formal education, like being enrolled in a class or in full-time schooling, I'd invite you to broaden the definition a bit and think more about your curiosity. I believe that, at our core, we are all curious beings. It's an important part of being human, because it's our curiosity that pushes us to adapt and evolve. So, as you look at the lists of traits, think about all areas of your current "educational" life, not just school.

able	detailed	hopeful	reasonable
academic	determined	humble	researcher
accomplished	devoted	informed	scholarly
ambitious	diligent	initiative	scientific
analyzer	disciplined	inquiring	self-motivated
artistic	driven	inquisitive	serious
aspiring	dynamic	intellectual	skilled
attentive	eager	intelligent	smart
avid	educated	interested	student
awakened	energetic	keen	studied
beginner	engaged	knowledgeable	studious
bright	enlightened	learner	talented
capable	enthusiastic	listener	teachable
clever	experienced	literary	teacherly
committed	expert	logical	thorough
competent	exploring	optimistic	thoughtful
confident	factual	practical	tireless
cooperative	focused	practicing	trained
creative	gifted	proficient	understanding
curious	goal-oriented	purposeful	well-read
dedicated	hard-working	questioning	wise

---

abandoning	cowardly	embarrassed	insincere
absentminded	cynical	fearful	intimidated
adrift	dense	half-hearted	irresponsible
aimless	detached	helpless	lazy
ambitionless	directionless	hopeless	lost
anxious	discouraging	hesitant	meaningless
apathetic	dishonest	idle	mediocre
apprehensive	dispassionate	ignorant	mindless
arrogant	disregarding	illiterate	misguided
awkward	disruptive	impatient	naïve
bored	distractable	inconsiderate	negative
careless	dogmatic	informal	neglectful
closed off	doubtful	inhibited	neutral
conceited	egotistical	insecure	passive

perfectionistic	self-important	unattainable	uninformed
pessimistic	shy	uncomfortable	uninterested
pompous	smug	uneasy	uninvolved
pretentious	thoughtless	uneducated	unskilled
purposeless	timid	unexceptional	untrained
self-conscious	unassertive	unimpressed	wary

How I am currently within my educational life:

_____ _____ _____ _____

_____ _____ _____ _____

_____ _____ _____ _____

_____ _____ _____ _____

Now, let's think about traits that describe how you are when you're being your Best Self in terms of your educational life. Think of times when you've been curious, asked questions, and explored more deeply topics that intrigue you, and times you've shared your passions with others. Maybe consider times you've pushed yourself to acquire a new skill, to understand a situation from several angles, or when you've used creative problem-solving at work or home.

Look at the list again and write down traits that represent your Best Self within your educational life.

Traits that describe me when
I'm being my Best Self in my educational life:

_____ _____ _____

_____ _____ _____

_____ _____ _____

_____

Now let's see your Best Self in action. When you are being your Best Self within your educational life, what exactly does that look like?

For example:

- If you selected "diligent" from the list of traits, perhaps you can recall a time when you took on a new project and you were on top of every detail, learning new information and adapting to each curveball that came your way.
- If you selected "informed" from the list of traits, maybe you remember a time when a doctor diagnosed you or someone in your family with an illness, and rather than feeling overwhelmed by your own lack of understanding, you chose to dive headfirst into research and made sure you were fully informed on the illness and all options for treatment.

Specific examples of how I behave in my educational life when I'm being my Best Self are:

1. _____

2. _____

3. _____

The Stories We Tell Ourselves

As I discussed in *Best Self*, I had a really tough time in school. As a result, I started to tell myself a story about how I wasn't good at learning, and I told myself that story so much that it became a deeply ingrained belief. That's called a limiting belief. It limited me from being able to reach my full potential. I created a wall in my brain that didn't exist until I put it there. I couldn't learn and retain information because I *believed* I couldn't. It took me a long time to figure that out, and then to release that limiting belief.

What kinds of limiting beliefs have you placed on yourself? Have you let a few life experiences completely color your view of yourself? Did you have a rough year in math, and now you believe you're practically incapable of basic addition and subtraction? Maybe your tennis coach told you you're uncoordinated, and you've never picked up a racket since? Was a certain English teacher particularly hard on you, and as a result, you've been telling yourself you're not a good writer? Did you always dream of doing something, but a limiting belief has stopped you from going for it? Think for a moment about any limiting beliefs you may have developed over time that have stood in your way of learning something.

My Limiting Beliefs:

1. _____

2. _____

3. _____

4. _____

Now that you see them written out, you have already taken huge strides. Those beliefs are figments of your imagination. There is no written rule saying that you must accept these beliefs and live your life by them. Right now, you can decide to be free of them. You can replace those beliefs with new beliefs about yourself. You can do what you *believe* you can do. Nothing more, and nothing less.

One of my clients told me a story recently about taking her five-year-old son to an indoor climbing gym. They wore safety harnesses that allowed them to gently come back down to the ground when they let go of the rungs. Her son had never made it to the top of this one particular section of the wall, and as he was climbing up, he started to say out loud, "I'm weak. I'm weak." She heard him and she lovingly replied, "Remember, you are what you say you are. If you want to make it to the top, you need to tell yourself that you are strong!"

So he immediately began saying out loud, "I'm strong. I'm strong." At first, it was just a whisper. Then, as he saw himself able to get higher and higher up that wall, he knew it was working. So he said it louder. "I'm strong! I'm STRONG!" Others in the gym turned to see what was going on as this little boy pushed his body harder and harder, and he surpassed the highest point he'd ever achieved on that wall. He smiled, and decided to keep going. Laser-focused on the top of that wall, where there was a button he'd push when he'd made it, he kept yelling with determination, "I'm strong!"

By the time he was two rungs away from the very top, a small crowd had gathered below. Everyone was cheering him on. He muscled his way up, and with great satisfaction and a "Woohoo!" he slapped that button as hard as he could. Everyone in that gym was inspired, and reminded that we are what we say we are. If he'd kept saying to himself, "I'm weak, I'm weak," do you think he ever would've made it to the top? No way. That outcome is predictable. But by changing his story, by shifting his belief from limiting to *unlimited*, he was able to do what had previously been impossible.

Now that you know your limiting beliefs, what are your new, unlimited beliefs about yourself? Write them here:

My Unlimited Beliefs:

1. _____

2. _____

3. _____

4. _____

How did that exercise feel? I hope you're seeing more clearly that you can learn, achieve, and acquire any knowledge, information, experience, skill, or ability that you set your mind to.

An Educational Experiment

It wasn't until later in life that I discovered the topics that really interested me, and then I was finally able to "make the grade." But it's important to remember that gaining knowledge is its own reward. What I want you to do is to spend time digging into your Best "Educational" Self and finding out what it is that fires you up!

Let's try a little experiment. What's a way that you could force yourself to get out of your comfort zone this week? It should be something that has no potentially harmful consequences. The idea here is to choose an activity you wouldn't normally think to do, and that might even terrify you. It should scare you at least a little bit. Here are some examples from people who have tried this with me:

- Enroll in a class that you have to attend at least once. It could be in auto repair, coding, cooking, language, art, etc.
- Sign up to teach a class of some sort. You are probably more qualified than you realize! For example, there are organizations that will have you read to children.
- Go to an event that is open to your community. It could be a senior mixer at the YMCA, a street festival, or a farmer's market. Make it a point to talk to a stranger!

This week, I will commit to getting out of my comfort zone by:

_____

_____

_____

Now, write down the result(s) of this activity. Did you learn something new? Did you meet and connect with a stranger?

_____

_____

_____

How did it feel getting out of your comfort zone?

_____

_____

_____

Do you feel you could take another risk like this in the future?

○ **YES**   ○ **NO**

Educational Sabotage

While limiting beliefs are perhaps the most pervasive way that we keep ourselves from evolving, there are other ways we sabotage our own growth. Sometimes we get caught up in the tide of our fast-paced lifestyle and become closed off to our educational pursuits. And sometimes we slip into a state of being a "know-it-all" and act as if we already have all the answers. That's typically because our Anti-Self has taken the reins.

Think about some ways that your Anti-Self tries to sabotage your opportunities to learn, evolve, stretch, and grow.

Write some examples here:

- _____

- _____

- _____

- _____

- _____

If your Best Self had been in charge, how would you have approached the above examples differently? Write it here:

- _____

- _____

- _____

- _____

- _____

Staying Accountable

I've found that the only thing more fun than learning something new is learning it alongside someone else so you can talk about it afterward! Think about your overall team and/or your inner circle of friends and family, and identify someone who would enjoy learning something new with you. Maybe you form a mini book club, and read a book simultaneously, and talk about it weekly, or perhaps you both enroll in a course of some kind. Whatever this might look like for you, I encourage you to stick to your educational goals by picking an accountability partner.

My accountability partner for my Education SPHERE is:

_____

Next, write down how you will ask them to help keep you on this new path. Will you ask them to help you say "yes" to new learning opportunities? Whatever your plan is, write it down here:

I will ask my accountability partner to help me by:

_____

_____

_____

BECOME A CASUAL LEARNER

In *Best Self*, I reminded you that learning can be casual. You don't always need a formal class in order to continue your education. Let's put that into action! Look back to page 190 in *Best Self: Be You, Only Better* and reconnect with the topics you wrote down. These were the topics you'd like to learn more about. Review the reasons why you hadn't yet spent time learning them. Since writing down that list, have you made headway on throwing out your excuses and finding ways to engage more with those subjects? If so, that's awesome! Keep it up, and keep adding to the list so you can continue to expand your knowledge.

If not, that's okay! This is your chance to reignite the fire within you and devise a plan for educating yourself, and thus evolving yourself. Remember, the subjects don't matter; these can seem random. Perhaps you are interested in Russian history, gardening, bread making, photography, or artificial intelligence. Seek out a book, podcast, audiobook, online tutorial, or documentary on the topic and learn something new, just for the fun of it—no tests or essays to follow! There's no pressure to become proficient or a subject-matter expert; the only requirement is that you approach the topic with curiosity and the intention to learn something new.

Afterward, tell someone else about what you learned, so the information stays fresh in your memory. And if you liked what you learned, find ways to dig deeper through additional resources. In other words, keep yourself steeped in learning mode!

Tracking Your Progress

After a couple of weeks, return to this chapter and check in with yourself to see whether you've made progress. Are there areas that require more of your attention? Write a few lines about how you've noticed yourself improving in your education life.

_____

_____

_____

_____

Be Your Best "Relationship" Self

No one thrives in isolation; we come to
know ourselves through others.
—*Best Self*

As much as society would have us believe that relationships are difficult, and that "it's complicated" is the status quo for most of us, I believe that relationships can actually be quite simple. The key is showing up as your Best Self within your relationships in order to preserve and protect balance within them, and prevent problems. Sometimes, especially when we're around people with whom we've become very comfortable, we drift away from our Best Self and become reactive. It's totally normal, and with the tools in this chapter and the Relationships chapter in *Best Self: Be You, Only Better*, you can maintain equilibrium.

Let's begin with these thought-provoking questions to get you into the mind-set. Write down what comes to mind when you read each question so that you can create a road map for topics you want to tackle while doing the work in this chapter.

1. Do you feel in touch with your principles or standards for living, and are you living them out within your relationships?

   - Do your values line up with those of your intimate partner?
   - How do your values compare to those of your family?

   Write your thoughts and answers here:

   _____

   _____

   _____

   _____

2. Are there unresolved issues within your family that directly involve and/or impact you?

   - Did you feel pressure from your family to behave in a certain way when you were young, and does that pressure still exist today?

- Are there negative moments from your childhood that are still with you today?
- Do you make decisions even today based on what your parents/ family would like you to do?

Write your thoughts and answers here:

_____

_____

_____

_____

3. Do you know, concretely, what you are willing to accept and not accept within an intimate relationship?

- Are you careful not to compromise your core values for an intimate relationship?
- Do you recognize that you and your partner do not have to be like-minded on every issue in order to have a good relationship?
- Do you acknowledge that you and your partner have flaws, but that you can have a great relationship regardless?
- Do you sometimes expect your partner to take responsibility for your happiness?
- Do you give to your partner that which you expect to receive?

Write your thoughts and answers here:

_____

_____

_____

_____

4. If you're a parent, do you feel you are showing up as your Best Self in the majority of your interactions with your child?

- Are you parenting in such a way as to foster your child's understanding of his or her own Best Self?
- Do you acknowledge that the most powerful role models in a child's life are his or her parents, and are you therefore thoughtful about the behavior you are modeling?
- Have you defined and outlined your family's priorities so that you can parent in a harmonious way?

Write your thoughts and answers here:

_____

_____

_____

_____

As you can see from those questions, and from the Relationships chapter in *Best Self*, we are covering your:

- family relationships
- intimate relationships
- relationship with your child (if you're a parent)

Throughout this chapter, you'll be doing exercises and some self-exploration to discover who your Best Self is when it comes to your relationships in all three of the above realms. Certainly, there are differences in how we relate to those in our family of origin, versus intimate relationships and our relationship with our child(ren). But in this workbook, I want to take you underneath those specifics to discover the values that are at the heart of how you relate to those closest to you, and to make the connection between your experiences as a child and those in your adult relationships. By taking an objective look at these aspects of yourself, you'll gain much more control over all of those key relationships in your life, and begin to feel like you're in the driver's seat rather than just at the mercy of someone else.

Evaluating Your Values

Returning to the Values Exercise on page 201 in *Best Self,* what are your top seven values? Write them here:

1. _____

2. _____

3. _____

4. _____

5. _____

6. _____

7. _____

The positive values represent your character strengths, while any values with a negative connotation are likely coming from your Anti-Self. If we've been living some aspect of our life steeped in our Anti-Self, certain negative values become engrained to the point that we begin to live by them. The goal is to identify those values, and discover how to move away from them and replace them with positive ones.

Gaining clarity around your core values will help you to see where your values either line up with or run contrary to those held by people in your immediate circles. Keep these in mind as you progress through this chapter, and make note if you realize that someone in your life has values that run contrary to your own.

Now, ask yourself these questions:

1. When I receive feedback from people in my life, does that feedback match up with my values? In other words, do others feel I am reflecting into the world those values that matter the most to me?

   • For instance, if one of my core values is optimism, do others view me as optimistic? If they were talking about me to someone who doesn't know me, would they describe me as someone who stands out as an optimist?
   ○ **YES**   ○ **NO**

If you answered "yes," what's a recent example of something you did or said that was a direct reflection of one of your core values?

_____

_____

_____

_____

If you answered "no," what is one way you could be proactive about making sure you are living out your core values in your everyday life?

_____

_____

_____

_____

_____

2. When you are facing some kind of adversity, which of your core values do you rely on to get you through to the other side?

- It is when the going gets tough that we most need to lean into our core values and allow them to navigate us through rough waters. Is this an area where you sometimes struggle? It's not always easy when the pressure is on to look within ourselves and act with integrity and authenticity.
- But putting some thought into it now, and deciding what kind of behavior you're going to exhibit when life throws you a curveball, can help make those decisions slightly easier when the time arrives.

Which characteristics sometimes interfere with your ability to operate from your core values (such as impatience or jealousy)?

- _____

- _____

- _____

- _____

If you could take a breath in times of stress and choose which of your values you're going to rely on to help you manage it, what are those values?

- _____

- _____

- _____

- _____

Remember—in order to take action, you must have insight. By connecting more deeply with your core values, you can begin to behave more consistently from within them.

Your Current Relationship Picture

Your core values apply broadly to your entire life, across all of your SPHERES. They are what matter to you the most. Now, let's drill down and look at who you are within your relationships specifically—these attributes that describe who you are and how you behave in relationships. There might be overlap with your top seven values; there might not be. But look at these lists of traits and then write down which ones accurately describe how you *currently* behave within your relationships. For the purposes of this exercise, choose traits that apply most universally to all of your relationships—familial, intimate, and parental.

acknowledges others	cooperative	forthright	leader
	courteous	friendly	lively
adventuresome	dedicated	fun-loving	loving
affectionate	discreet	functional	magnanimous
agreeable	dutiful	gallant	mature
amiable	dynamic	generous	modest
amicable	empathetic	gentle	nurturing
appreciative	empowered	genuine	optimistic
approachable	enchanting	giving	patient
attentive	encouraging	good-natured	perceptive
calm	enthusiastic	gracious	personable
cheery	ethical	grateful	persuasive
collaborative	exciting	helpful	philanthropic
compassionate	fair	hospitable	playful
conciliatory	faithful	humorous	polished
confident	fearless	inspiring	popular
connective	flexible	intuitive	principled
cool	forgiving	kind	protective

rational
reasonable
relaxed
reliable
respectful
responsive
romantic
safe
sage

sanguine
selfless
sensitive
sociable
sophisticated
spontaneous
steadfast
subtle
supportive

sweet
sympathetic
tenacious
tender
thoughtful
tolerant
trusting
trustworthy
unassuming

uncomplaining
understanding
undogmatic
warm
watchful
welcoming

---

abrasive
abrupt
angry
anxious
apathetic
argumentative
arrogant
artificial
awkward
bitter
boring
brutal
calculating
callous
cantankerous
charmless
clingy
cold
complaintive
compulsive
conceited
conformist
cowardly
crass

critical
crude
cynical
deceitful
demanding
devious
disagreeable
discouraging
dishonest
disloyal
disrespectful
disruptive
distractable
dogmatic
domineering
duplicitous
egotistical
fixed
follower
gloomy
greedy
gullible
hateful
haughty

hostile
impatient
inconsiderate
indiscreet
inhibited
insecure
insincere
insulting
intolerant
intoxicated
irritable
jealous
judgmental
loud
malicious
mannerless
mean
moody
narcissistic
needy
negative
obnoxious
overly opinionated
paranoid

passive
perfectionist
perverse
pessimistic
petty
pompous
possessive
resentful
rigid
rude
sarcastic
sassy
self-centered
sinister
tactless
tense
unapologetic
unappreciative
unfriendly
ungrateful
unpleasant
unwelcoming
uptight
vain

How I am currently within my
Relationship SPHERE:

_____   _____   _____   _____

_____   _____   _____   _____

Next, look at the same list of traits, and identify ones that accurately describe how you are in your relationships when you are being your Best Self. What does being completely and totally yourself look like? Think about times when you weren't allowing the past to color your current mood or reactions to another person. Or think about times when you were fully relaxed, not carrying baggage around from your workday or other stressors, just being fully present and engaged in the moment with a close friend.

For example, are you patient, warm, and selfless when you're being your Best Self? Are you able to lighten any situation with your humor, and able to find the silver lining no matter what? Think about all the different traits that describe how you are when you're behaving from a place of authenticity with those you love and care about.

How I am when I'm being my Best Self within my relationships:

_____   _____   _____

_____   _____   _____

_____   _____   _____

Is the picture becoming clearer of who you are, and who you are capable of being within your relationships? Are you noticing any patterns? A good way to help you recognize these patterns in a more tangible way is to think about specific examples of these traits playing out in your life.

For example:

- If you selected "safe" from the list of positive traits, perhaps you enjoy being that safe place to fall for those you love—anytime they are worn out or worn down, you are always there to hold them close and help them feel secure in the knowledge that it's all going to be okay.
- If you selected "adventuresome" from the list of traits, an example might be when you planned a trip with your intimate partner, which included several activities that were outside the norm of your daily life, and together you experienced a great adventure that strengthened your bond.

Specific examples of my Best Self traits in action within my relationships are:

1. _____

2. _____

3. _____

Now, think about ways in which you can allow your Best Self to take the lead more often within your relationships. Consider recent scenarios that have occurred within your family, intimate, or parental relationships when you may not have shown up as your Best Self, and what you would have done differently if you had been your Best Self.

Scenario 1:

What happened? _____

    + How I reacted: _____

_____

    = Outcome: _____

What happened? _____

    + How my Best Self would have reacted: _____

_____

    = Predicted Outcome: _____

Scenario 2:

What happened? _____

+ How I reacted: _____

_____

= Outcome: _____

What happened? _____

+ How my Best Self would have reacted: _____

_____

= Predicted Outcome: _____

Scenario 3:

What happened? _____

+ How I reacted: _____

_____

= Outcome: _____

What happened? _____

+ How my Best Self would have reacted: _____

_____

= Predicted Outcome: _____

Your Attachments

Our family relationships are the first ways we learn to communicate and connect with others. Our capacity for resiliency has its roots in those earliest relationships. At the CAST Centers, my dual diagnosis rehabilitation center in West Hollywood, where we work with people on everything from anxiety and depression to addiction—both in person and online as a telehealth forum—we use something called the CAST Alignment Model. In it, we explore our attachment patterns of behavior and the impact they have on our lives today.

There are two primary types of attachment: secure and insecure. Secure attachments imply a system in which the attachment figure, usually a parent or caregiver, is seen as accessible and responsive when needed. Insecure attachments imply a system in which the responsiveness of the caregiver cannot be assumed, and the child's fundamental needs are often not met. This drives the child to adopt a strategy to compensate for and cope with the perceived unresponsiveness of the parent or caregiver. This could manifest as disruptive, attention-seeking behavior. Alternatively, it could lead a person in a positive direction, to teaching them to develop certain survival skills.

Let's explore your own attachments.

- Do you feel you formed a close emotional bond with your parent(s) or primary caregivers? In other words, did you perceive that they met your needs and gave you a secure base from which you could safely explore the world?

  ○ YES   ○ NO

- If you answered "yes," then you likely experienced a secure attachment as a child.
- If you answered "no," then you likely experienced an insecure attachment as a child.
- If you had an insecure attachment, what are some ways you think that has played out in your adult relationships?
  - For example, do you find yourself seeking out romantic relationships that somehow duplicate your experiences or negative emotions you experienced as a child, despite how painful?

Write your thoughts and answers here:

_____

_____

_____

_____

If you've come to the realization that you experienced an insecure attachment to your parents or caregivers as a child, and that there might be repercussions on your relationships today, there is hope. There are plenty of people who have lived through insecure attachments and discovered ways they can have healthy, fulfilling relationships as adults. Yes, it takes effort, but it's completely achievable. Here are some tools:

TOOL 1: You can create more awareness by identifying your needs in any given relationship.

- In this process, make sure your needs are realistic, and that you aren't seeking something from someone else that only you can give yourself.
- For example, if you think you need to be accepted by others, the truth is, you really only need to accept yourself. Or if you're looking for other people to make you happy, that is not their responsibility. You control your own happiness.

What are needs in your relationships that aren't currently being met? This can apply to familial or intimate relationships:

_____

_____

_____

TOOL 2: You can engage in healthy communication with the other person.

- Rather than keeping your feelings and needs to yourself, find ways to communicate them effectively to your partner.
- Choose moments when you are both calm and not juggling other responsibilities. Good communication requires attentiveness from both parties.

Write down your ideas for more effectively communicating within your relationships:

_____

_____

_____

TOOL 3: You can set healthy boundaries with others so that you never feel as though others are taking advantage of you.

- Instead of letting others walk all over you, speak to you in a disrespectful manner, or take from you without giving back, you can choose to stand up for yourself, say "no" more often, and require others to treat you with respect.
- As my friend Dr. Phil always says, you teach people how to treat you. If you aren't setting up healthy boundaries and expectations for others, they will (purposely or not) take advantage of you.

What relationship(s) in your life currently require a boundary?

_____

_____

_____

Write down some ways you can set healthy boundaries in your familial, intimate, and/or parental relationships:

_____

_____

_____

TOOL 4: You can work on managing the feelings that arise when you might not get what you want or expect from others.

- This starts by being honest with yourself about what you are expecting from people and relationships. Are you expecting someone to do something that is outside of their ability, or that you haven't made clear to them?
- Other people, even intimate partners, are not mind readers, so if you expect something of them, you must communicate that information.
- If you often find yourself feeling hurt or let down by others who are close to you, then take a moment to reflect on whether your expectations are unreasonable or unsaid.

Write down ways you can manage your expectations and the feelings that arise when they are not met:

_____

_____

_____

Subtle Shifts

Everyone experiences moments of adversity within their relationships. Sometimes we must make the difficult decision to part ways with someone in our life because the relationship has simply become too toxic. But if you can resolve to do everything in your power to show up as your Best Self in your relationships, you will likely begin to notice subtle shifts within them. Or it might even surprise you when those shifts aren't so subtle, and things get back on a healthy track faster than anticipated. The point is that you can only control your actions, so if you can let go of trying to change or control the other person and just focus on yourself, then you're already winning.

Choosing someone to whom you can be accountable to behaving as your Best Self is not to be taken lightly. You should select someone who can remain objective, who isn't biased one way or another, who can be discreet, and who has your best interests at heart. You may want to pick a different person to whom you're accountable for each of the various relationships you're working on. Write down your accountability partner(s) here:

My accountability partner(s) for my Relationships is/are:

_____

_____

_____

Next, write down how you will ask each person to help keep you on your new path. Will he or she help you manage your expectations and your feelings when they are not met? Will he or she check in with you each morning to help you set your intentions for how you're parenting your child? Whatever your plan is, write it down here:

I will ask my accountability partner(s) to help me by:

_____

_____

_____

Tracking Your Progress

After a couple of weeks, return to this chapter and check in with yourself to see whether you've improved in your relationships. Look back at the questions I asked at the very beginning of this chapter.

Do you feel you've made progress? Are there areas that require more of your attention? Write a few lines about how you've noticed yourself improving in your relationships.

_____

_____

_____

_____

Be Your Best "Employment" Self

I believe that if you stay rooted in your authenticity while earning
your living, life will surprise you beyond your wildest dreams.
—*Best Self*

Yes, this is the chapter about your employment, but if you aren't currently employed, have no plans to work, or you're retired, before you skip to the next chapter, I'd like to encourage you to look at the exercises in this chapter and think about how they apply to your life in some other way. For instance, if you are involved with a volunteer or philanthropic organization, many of the principles discussed here can be exceedingly helpful to you in those arenas. Further, if you are managing your finances or receiving earnings from other outlets besides work, these insights can be valuable to you as well. And even if your partner earns the household income, I'm willing to bet that the two of you sometimes discuss what's going on within that business, and this chapter could be useful in that context as well.

If you are currently employed in any capacity, are you able to show up as your Best Self while you're at work? For many, it's a struggle. I believe this is partly because we are taught from an early age that we need to root our identity in *what* we do for a living. We're asked, "*What* do you want to be when you grow up?" rather than "*Who* are you?" We focus so much on figuring out what we're going to do to make a living that we spend little or no time exploring who we authentically are so that we can then ensure that our livelihood is in alignment with our Best Self. The result is often a lack of fulfillment within our careers. And when you think about the number of hours we spend working over the course of our lives, it's a tragedy that we wouldn't be spending that time feeling connected to our passions and our purpose.

Within this workbook chapter, I encourage you to focus on discovering your "why." It could be that you'll discover how to live out your "why" within your existing employment, or you might find that it's time to consider a pivot in your career. Don't allow fear of the unknown or anxiety around change to creep in while you're doing this exploration. All we're doing right now is visualizing what your employment *could* look like. It's important that you are willing to deeply imagine the possibilities. So often, we stand in our own way of creating an amazing, fulfilling life because we're so steeped in our own fear. Don't block your ability to have your Best Self career.

As you begin this leg of your journey, keep your answers to the following questions in mind:

1. In *Best Self*, we talked about how we are all artists. In what ways are you able to express your own form of "art" within your career?

_____

_____

_____

• How is the work that you do helping you to grow in positive ways?

_____

_____

_____

• What are a couple of ways that you are utilizing and strengthening your own unique skills and talents through your work?

_____

_____

_____

• What are some examples of how your work stimulates your
  creativity?

  _____

  _____

  _____

• How would you describe the connection between your
  passion(s) and your job/career?

  _____

  _____

  _____

2. In what ways does your work energize and excite you?

  _____

  _____

  _____

- When you're getting ready for or on your way to work each day, what is going through your mind?

_____

_____

_____

- What are some recent examples of how your work feels rewarding to you?

_____

_____

_____

- In what way(s) are you contributing to the world in a positive way through your work?

_____

_____

_____

3. If you ever struggle in an aspect (or several aspects) of your work, how does that play out for you?

_____

_____

_____

_____

- When are the times that you do not like your job?

_____

_____

_____

- How do you feel about the people with whom you work?

_____

_____

_____

- How do you feel at the end of your workday? Do you feel like work has completely zapped all of your energy, or do you feel like you have plenty of gas left in your tank to spend time with family and accomplish personal tasks?

_____

_____

_____

- In what ways does your work inspire you?

_____

_____

_____

4. What feelings surrounded money when you were growing up?

_____

_____

_____

- Have you experienced any traumatic events or stressors that were related to money? If so, what were they?

  _____

  _____

  _____

- What are your limiting beliefs around your ability to make money?

  _____

  _____

  _____

- How do you feel about how much money you're making at your current job?

  _____

  _____

  _____

Envisioning Your Best Self Career

In the book *Best Self*, I asked you to think about what your Best Self would like to do for work, in an ideal world. We talked about the type of work that you'd like to be doing where you'd feel like you're using your gifts, expressing your art, and feeling productive and rewarded by the work you do. Let's revisit that exercise, and then build upon it.

1. First, take a deep breath and allow your body and mind to completely relax.

2. Next, before you think about a specific job, think about how you would like to feel while you are working. What comes to mind?

- *While working, I would like to feel:*

_____

_____

_____

(Example: While working, I would like to feel challenged but not overwhelmed, excited about the work I'm generating, and at peace rather than under pressure.)

3. Now, think about what types of activities are most fulfilling to you, that make you feel like you are living out your purpose for living.

   • *I feel most fulfilled when I am:*

   _____

   _____

   _____

   _____

   (Example: I feel most fulfilled when I am caring for others and providing a service that makes someone else feel better.)

4. The final step in this process is to consider the work you are currently doing and see if it lines up with your answers above. If it doesn't, that's okay. But now you are empowered with an understanding of what you want out of a career, and you can begin to work toward creating that, whether it is:

   • through a "side hustle," where you create time in your schedule for work that is fulfilling to you
   • by first volunteering during some of your free time in order to experience what it is you're looking for
   • by finding ways within your current job or company to feel more fulfilled

It might be time for you to start searching for a new position doing something that is in line with your Best Self. If that's the case, then spend as much time as you can researching your next move, because you don't want to waste any more time doing something for a living that isn't aligned with your Best Self.

Your Current Employment Picture

Let's start by getting a complete picture of your current professional life. Be honest with yourself as you look through these lists of traits, and select the ones, or write new ones, that accurately describe how you currently think and behave with regard to your job.

able	confident	enthusiastic	intentional
accomplished	conscientious	ethical	kind
achiever	content	excited	knowledgeable
administrative	creative	experienced	leader
admired	dedicated	expert	limitless
ambitious	detailed	focused	listener
aspiring	determined	formal	manageable
attentive	devoted	friendly	meaningful
avid	diligent	fulfilled	methodical
balanced	disciplined	genuine	missional
bright	driven	goal-oriented	moral
businesslike	dynamic	grateful	motivated
capable	eager	hardworking	optimistic
clever	efficient	helpful	organized
committed	encouraging	hopeful	passionate
competent	energized	humble	persevering

personable	proud	self-aware	thorough
poised	punctual	smart	trained
practical	purposeful	stable	valuable
pragmatic	qualified	successful	visionary
proactive	reasonable	supportive	vital
problem-solver	relational	systematic	willing
productive	resourceful	teachable	worthy
professional	respectful	teacherly	
proficient	rewarding	team-player	

---

abandoning	discouraging	informal	pessimistic
absentminded	dishonest	inhibited	pompous
adrift	disregarding	insecure	pressured
aimless	disruptive	insignificant	pretentious
ambitionless	distracted	insincere	procrastinator
anxious	doubtful	intimidated	purposeless
apathetic	dramatic	irresponsible	restless
apprehensive	dull	isolated	rude
argumentative	egotistical	jealous	scattered
arrogant	embarrassed	lazy	self-conscious
avoidant	exhausted	limited	shy
awkward	fearful	lost	struggling
bored	half-hearted	meaningless	tactless
careless	helpless	mediocre	timid
complaining	hesitant	micromanager	toxic
conceited	hopeless	mindless	uncomfortable
concerned	idle	misguided	unethical
cowardly	immoral	narcissistic	unmotivated
cynical	impatient	negative	unorganized
demanding	impersonal	neglectful	unprofessional
demeaning	inconsiderate	nitpicking	unsuccessful
deprived	indifferent	overwhelmed	wandering
detached	inexperienced	passive	workaholic
directionless	inferior	perfectionist	worthless

How I am currently within my Employment SPHERE:

_____   _____   _____

_____   _____   _____

_____   _____   _____

_____   _____   _____

_____   _____   _____

Now, let's take a moment to connect the traits you see in yourself within your employment to your actual behavior with regard to your job. If you selected "perfectionist," for example, perhaps there's been a time when your need for perfection in any given task has driven you to be stubborn, or even unkind to yourself or others at work. Or if you selected "overwhelmed," maybe you can think of a time when you just wanted to walk away from your job, or you've felt extremely emotional because it just felt like you'd never be able to accomplish everything that has been asked of you. Be specific in the examples you write down, as they can really help illuminate what your feelings and behaviors at work are telling you about your current employment experience.

Real-world examples of how I currently feel, think, and behave at work:

Example 1: _____

Example 2: _____

Example 3: _____

Next, look at the same lists of traits and identify ones that describe how you behave within your employment when you are being your Best Self.

So, if you selected "administrative" from the list of positive traits, perhaps you take pride in your ability to stay organized and keep your workplace running smoothly and efficiently, and you've even received compliments or acknowledgment from your boss or coworkers. If you selected "purposeful" from the list of traits, maybe you are motivated by your company's mission and, though the work is not always easy or without frustration, you feel you are making a significant contribution to your community.

How I am when I'm being my Best Self within my employment:

_____   _____   _____

_____   _____   _____

_____   _____   _____

_____   _____   _____

Taking the Focus off More Money

I have worked with countless clients who say they are unhappy in their careers, and when I ask them, "What would make you happier?" they reply, "If I made more money." That's a mistake. It's so easy to blame your unhappiness on lack of financial reward, but the truth is, if you were feeling truly aligned with your Best Self in your job, you wouldn't be so concerned about money. When your focus is solely on your paycheck, your attitude can very quickly become an endless merry-go-round of resentment, feeling unappreciated, and being jealous of those who are making more. This resentment is then reflected in your output, and maybe you aren't getting promoted as a result, and then the feeling gets even worse, and so on. Not a pretty picture, and not how you want to spend the majority of your week!

The more you can shift your focus off the money you are making and on to ways you can weave passion and purpose into your work, the happier you will feel. Work just happens to be the thing that generates money.

Here are some questions to ask yourself:

1. When you're at work, or thinking about your job, does your mind inevitably zero in on how much you're making?

   ○ **YES**　○ **NO**

If yes, then what are some thoughts you can shift your mind toward instead?

_____

_____

_____

2. What kinds of changes can you make today in order to think of ways your career fulfills you, other than financially?

_____

_____

_____

YOUR BEST SELF SAVINGS STRATEGY

Finances are universally one of the biggest stressors in people's lives. As Dr. Phil always says, "You don't solve money problems with money." You behave your way to success in life, and that applies to money management. No matter how deep you feel in a financial hole, it is always possible to begin to save money. Yes, you need to be organized and strategic if you're tackling debt, but part of that strategy must be to set aside some amount of money on a regular basis. It doesn't have to be a lot, especially at first. But the more you see yourself able to save for the future, the less stress and pressure you will feel around your earnings. Your Best Self always looks out for your future self, and that means doing whatever you can to create financial savings for a "rainy day" or retirement. Preparation reduces anxiety.

This doesn't have to be a complicated process, either! You just have to start. If you don't already have a savings account, go open one today and start setting aside money on a routine basis, at least monthly.

How much can you commit to saving on a monthly basis today?

$_____

The "Yes" Key to Career Freedom

I was recently at a party with someone, and when I asked what he did, he said, "You know, I've been at work all day, I really don't want to talk about work." It was very apparent to me that he did not love his job. At the end of my workday, I enjoy talking about projects I'm involved in, and ideas that I've been having. That's the way I think we should all feel about our careers!

I've found that clients who say they are miserable in their careers usually feel that way because they don't have enough freedom. Even though they may start out by talking about wanting to make more money, or wanting to be more respected, or hoping for that next big promotion—when we get to the heart of the issue, it's about freedom. What we really seek is some autonomy over our lives. We want to be able to have some flexibility in our schedules, some decision-making capabilities around which projects we're working on, etc. So, how does one achieve that? The answer is simpler than it might seem. Say *yes*.

When someone at your job asks you to go above and beyond in some way, or to take on something extra, or to do a task on a weekend, do you immediately say "yes" and jump at the opportunity? Or are you more likely to draw a boundary, explain that it would cut into personal time, or that you aren't available for work on the weekends, or that it's "not your job"? Do you think that if you set a precedent with your boss that he or she will soon be taking advantage of you?

Write your thoughts and answers to those questions here:

_____

_____

_____

I can tell you this from four different perspectives—as a life coach, as an employer, as an employee (which I've been in many different organizations), and as a mentee—saying "yes" will ultimately get you to the level of freedom that you desire. But if you stay in that "no" mentality, it's either going to take a lot longer or it might never happen for you. When you're willing to be the employee that juggles multiple tasks, always shows up, and always says "yes," you will find that you will move up the ladder much faster. Leaders are always looking for superstars, and superstars always say yes.

I remember talking to an employee on a Friday, and we both had meetings we had to get to, and I asked if I could call her to follow up over the weekend. It wasn't something I'd ever requested before, but I knew we were both feeling inspired about a new project we were going to be starting, and I didn't want to lose momentum. She paused, and then said, "I have a lot of errands this weekend. Let's just talk on Monday." Perhaps that's an appropriate boundary in terms of her belief around what it means to be an employee, but that's just not how it works when you're working for me. If she had wanted to work for a traditional outpatient center, her boundary would be just fine, but for someone who has as many projects and opportunities as I do, you have to be willing to show up when needed. I had been looking forward to investing time into her, but when she prioritized errands over that, I wasn't feeling nearly as motivated. She thought she was just setting a boundary. But she didn't look at it from my perspective. That's what I encourage you to do. Walk a day in your boss's shoes and think about how your behavior is coming across to him or her. Are you showing commitment, excitement, inspiration, and dedication?

I had another employee who worked in operations and had already pulled a full shift, but when the front desk receptionist had to go home to her sick daughter, my operations manager didn't even hesitate—she just sat down behind the desk and started answering phones. It's that kind of attitude that helps you grow as an employee, and helps the company grow as well.

When was the last time you did something that "wasn't your job," and not just for the recognition?

You can always tell a good employee, and an employee who has a desire to grow and achieve not by what they say, but by what they do. You gain freedom by saying yes, and taking action.

Asking for Help

You're not always going to have the answers, but luckily, you don't need to in order to have your Best Self career. What *is* required is a tenacious spirit, which means you're willing to do whatever it takes to find the answers you need in order to do your job. Creative problem-solving means doing your research. Sometimes that means looking on the Internet, other times it means asking a coworker for guidance. Doing your research might even mean asking your boss for clarity. You need to be able to say, "I don't know how to do that, but I'm certainly willing to learn." Asking for help isn't a sign of weakness—it's smart!

What's an example of a time when you could have saved time or done a better job by asking for help or actively seeking out the answers you needed? Write it here:

_____

_____

_____

What would have been a better course of action?

_____

_____

_____

There also might be times when you notice an inefficiency in the way some aspect of your company runs, and you make a suggestion to improve it. Maybe you see that the phone system is outdated and doesn't work well, so you find out about a new system that would be better. Or it could be as simple as reorganizing your desk so that you're able to accomplish more in a shorter amount of time.

What's a way you could help improve efficiency in your job or organization?

_____

_____

_____

_____

Next Steps

Write down three areas you've noticed you need to improve within your employment, and three corresponding changes you can make immediately to either show up as your Best Self in your current job, or to move toward identifying a job that is more closely connected to who you are authentically:

What I've Noticed: **Immediate Action I Can Take:**

1. _____   _____

2. _____   _____

3. _____   _____

I believe that everyone should have someone they consider a mentor. This should be someone you look up to, who is their Best Self in their job, and who is passionate about lifting others up to achieve their career goals. It might be someone who works in a totally different industry, or it might be someone within your own organization.

My accountability partner in the area of my Employment is:

_____

Next, write down how you will ask them to help keep you on track. Will you ask them to check in with you each week about a looming work deadline that you've been dreading? Will you ask them to keep you in mind if they hear of potential job openings for which you would be a good fit? If they are a fellow coworker, will you ask them to give you honest feedback so you can identify areas of improvement? Whatever your plan is, write it down here:

I will ask my accountability partner to help me by:

_____

_____

_____

_____

_____

Tracking Your Progress

After a couple of weeks, return to this chapter and check in with your-self to see if you've kept the forward momentum in your employment. Do you feel you've made progress? Are there areas that require more of your attention? Write a few lines about how you've noticed yourself improving in your professional life.

_____

_____

_____

_____

Be Your Best "Spiritual" Self

I believe our spiritual life underpins everything else in life. I
think of your Best Self as actually being your spiritual self.
Your spiritual self is the place within you from which all
goodness and light radiates outward. It is where you form
your integrity, values, and how you treat other people.

—*Best Self*

When people hear the word "spiritual," they make a lot of as-
sumptions. It can be a very loaded word. For many people, the
word "spiritual" stirs deeply rooted emotions because of past experiences they have come to associate with religion. Some of those experiences may have been profoundly enlightening. Others may have been
detrimental. What floats to the surface for you when you think of the
word "spiritual"? Ponder that for just a moment.

Some of that baggage can muddy the waters for us when we are doing work within our spiritual life. And the truth is, when we nurture our spiritual life, we will experience benefits within all of our other SPHERES. So, before you approach the work within this chapter, let's pause for a moment and remove all the attachments we have to the idea of spirituality.

Imagine that your spirituality is a beautiful tree, and there are all kinds of memories and ideas dangling from the branches. Walk up to the tree, and gently remove each hanging memento from your past and place them to the side. One by one, just take them down until all that's left is the tree, its branches strong, its leaves a vibrant green, its roots extending deep into the earth. It sways easily in the breeze, yet remains strong and rooted even in the winds. This is your spirit. This is *you*.

Now, with all of those encumbrances gone, let's delve into who you are within your spiritual life. Be kind to yourself as you walk through each step of this process. Use these questions to guide your exploration.

1. What do you believe about God/the universe?

_____

_____

_____

_____

- What role does faith play in your everyday life?

  _____

  _____

  _____

- What role does faith play for you when you are faced with adversity?

  _____

  _____

  _____

- When life gets stressful, disappointing, or overwhelming, how do you get through it?

  _____

  _____

  _____

- How do you maintain spirituality in your life? (that is, meditating, praying, attending religious services, discussing faith with a friend, volunteering, reading scripture, spending time in nature, attending yoga classes, or whatever way feels authentic to you)

_____

_____

_____

_____

2. Part of having faith that things will work out for you means letting go of control to some degree. What are some ways in which you struggle with the concept of "control" in your life?

_____

_____

_____

_____

- What are some examples of when/if you worry about the future?

  _____

  _____

  _____

- How does fear or anxiety about making decisions in your life impact your daily life?

  _____

  _____

  _____

- In what ways do you beat yourself up about choices you've made in the past?

  _____

  _____

  _____

3. Do you subscribe to the belief that things happen *for* you, not *to* you? If so, what's an example of that playing out in your life? If not, what do you believe instead?

_____

_____

_____

• Describe a time in your life when something did not go your way, but ultimately led to an unforeseen opportunity.

_____

_____

_____

4. In *Best Self*, we talked about how sometimes people will choose to stay in their current suffering out of fear of the unknown. What's an example of a time when you chose to continue suffering rather than taking a risk?

_____

_____

_____

• In what way(s) are you choosing suffering over change
right now?

_____

_____

_____

If you really dug deep when you were answering those questions, then you might have some new questions of your own. Perhaps you experienced some epiphanies or connected dots in your spiritual life that you hadn't previously been aware of. If that's the case, then let's investigate a bit more by writing down any patterns emerging in your spiritual life. What are some areas that you now realize might benefit from some change? Here is some guidance to get you thinking in this way.

1. What, if any, new questions about your spiritual life came to mind as you wrote your answers to the four questions above?

_____

_____

_____

2. What is a pattern or theme you noticed in your answers to the four questions above?

_____

_____

_____

3. Based on your answers to those questions, what is an area within your spiritual life that you feel might benefit from some change in your thoughts, feelings, or behaviors?

_____

_____

_____

Now, as you continue through the work in the rest of this chapter, keep these observations in mind so that you can cultivate your unique spiritual journey.

Snapshot of Your Current Spiritual Life

Our spirituality isn't "set it and forget it"; it's something to be nurtured and carefully maintained through the years. It evolves with us over the course of our lives. You may have had one set of beliefs about a higher power or the universe at an earlier point in your life that has since changed into a different set of beliefs. As you look at the list of attributes below, think about where you are right now in your spiritual life. Select words from the list, or write new words that apply.

able	creative	grateful	reliant
accepting	decisive	harmonious	religious
agreeable	dedicated	hopeful	resolved
aligned	deserving	humble	restful
alive	determined	independent	satisfied
artistic	devoted	inquisitive	searching
aspiring	devout	intentional	self-aware
assured	diligent	joyful	self-motivated
attentive	disciplined	listener	sensing
available	encouraging	missional	sensitive
awakened	energetic	nurturing	serene
aware	engaged	observant	soulful
believing	enlightened	open	spiritual
bright	enriched	optimistic	steady
calm	enthusiastic	peaceful	sure
certain	expecting	persevering	thoughtful
clear	exploring	positive	trusting
comfortable	faithful	powerful	understanding
complete	focused	practicing	valuable
composed	free	prosperous	willing
connected	fulfilled	purposeful	worthy
consistent	generous	quiet	
content	genuine	reasonable	

afraid	dispirited	indifferent	pessimistic
agitated	dissatisfied	insecure	pressured
anxious	doubtful	jealous	purposeless
apathetic	down	judgmental	resistant
apprehensive	dreadful	lazy	restless
avoidant	dull	lifeless	sad
bored	empty	manipulated	scared
burdened	exhausted	meaningless	self-conscious
careless	fearful	melancholy	strained
cowardly	fretful	mindless	stressed
cynical	gloomy	miserable	tense
dejected	grieving	moody	timid
denying	helpless	negative	tired
depleted	hesitant	neglectful	troubled
depressed	hopeless	nervous	uncertain
despondent	hurt	obsessed	unhappy
detached	idle	obstinate	worried
directionless	impatient	offended	worthless
discontented	inattentive	overwhelmed	
discouraged	inconsolable	passive	

How I am currently within my Spiritual SPHERE:

_____   _____   _____

_____   _____   _____

_____   _____   _____

Now, think about those times in your spiritual life when you've been fully aligned with your Best Self, and look at the list again. Write down traits that represent your Best Self within your spiritual life.

How I am when I'm being my
Best Self in my spiritual life:

_____   _____   _____

_____   _____   _____

_____   _____   _____

_____   _____   _____

_____   _____   _____

Now, let's consider your Best Self in action. When you are being your Best Self within your spiritual life, what exactly does that look like?

- For example, maybe you selected "hopeful" from the list of traits because you have stayed optimistic during a particularly difficult season for your family rather than giving in to a sense of hopelessness or despair.
- Or if you selected "observant" from the list of traits, maybe you have started spending more time outside in nature, and it has caused you to slow down and notice things you never would have before—like the vibrant flowers in the neighbor's yard, or the sounds of birds chirping in the trees.

Specific examples of how I behave in my spiritual life when I'm being my Best Self are:

1. _____

2. _____

3. _____

Change Your Gr-Attitude

Gratitude has been talked about so much that it's practically lost its meaning. Here's the deal: if you can create time and space within your life to practice being grateful, you will experience not-so-subtle shifts in your spiritual life. And if you're noticing that the ways you express your gratitude begin feeling routine, then it's time to switch it up.

The important aspect of any expression of gratitude is that it feels authentic. You shouldn't be focused on other things, such as answering a text message from a friend, driving on the freeway, watching TV, or anything else that distracts you. In order to reap the benefits of gratitude, close your eyes, and envision in your mind's eye the person, place, thing, idea, or feeling for which you are grateful, and then really *feel* the wave of gratitude wash completely over you. Commit fully to that feeling of gratitude. Give it your undivided attention.

Recognizing the people and things that mean something to you, that help you, that you have been given or that you have earned—it's something that is easily overlooked. And yet the power of that appreciation is unending.

What are some things in your life for which you wish to express your "Gr-Attitude"?

- _____

- _____

- _____

What are a couple of new ways you can express your deep appreciation for those things?

- _____

- _____

- _____

Spiritual Growth Through Acceptance

Faith has a lot to do with acceptance. This is something that many people struggle with, but knowing that there are some circumstances we are powerless to change, and accepting those circumstances and then growing from them, is essentially what faith looks like. We can either choose to live in the painful belief that we can't change, or we can choose to accept it, move through, and grow away from it.

Is there something in your life that you've had a hard time accepting? If so, write it here:

_____

_____

_____

Was there ever a time when something occurred that you didn't want or expect, but it ended up okay in the end? Or perhaps it even turned you in a new and better direction?

_____

_____

_____

When we hit a brick wall in our lives, one option is to change our course. Sure, we can choose to keep bumping up against that wall again and again, but pivoting in a new direction is often the option that leads us right to where we're meant to be.

How can you accept and move through something that's been difficult for you? Be specific in your answer.

_____

_____

_____

What is a possible positive outcome of this difficult situation?

_____

_____

_____

You can return to this acceptance exercise anytime you're faced with a challenge, adversity, or any kind of unexpected circumstances. This is one way to further develop your spiritual life because it helps you to see that even though you can't control every outcome, you can still be okay. The universe has your best interests at heart, and even in the darkest moments, you can still choose to see the light.

Spiritual Growth Through Connection

Your spiritual life shouldn't be something that you cultivate in isolation. Community is a powerful help in spiritual growth. When people come together to express or discuss their spirituality, incredible things can happen. This looks different for everyone, of course. For some, this might mean attending a regular yoga class, where a dozen or more people are working to deepen their mind-body-spirit connection together in one space. For others, a spiritual practice could look like a religious service, such as within a church, synagogue, mosque, or other place of worship. It could even translate to meeting a friend for coffee and sharing your faith with each other.

Another way we can grow spiritually is by serving other people. There is true power within the spiritual stirring we feel when we are in service to others. By volunteering your time and energy to help someone else, you are opening a window into your soul, and pouring in love. When we are selflessly giving to others, we receive so much more than we can imagine. Bottom line—when we do good, we feel good. There are endless ways in which we can use our own gifts, talents, and abilities to help people—and each is as unique as we are. Once you open your mind and heart to the idea, you'll be surprised how many opportunities will appear.

Our subconscious often makes excuses for not creating spiritual space in our lives. Sometimes the practice isn't high on the list of priorities. If you think back to when humans were primarily living in tribes, maintaining strong community connection was an essential aspect of survival. By working together, groups of people were able to stay strong and safe from outside threats. But as we have evolved, we have moved further apart from one another. We aren't "communing" as we used to, and I think we are seeing the detrimental effects of this manifesting in a multitude of ways. The truth is, if we could make an effort to return to a stronger sense of community, and to allow ourselves to be open and share our spiritual selves, we would see a lot less depression, anxiety, isolation, and even suicide. It's that significant.

Right now, consider some ways that you can easily fit more community connection into your lifestyle in order to help bolster your spiritual development. Be specific in your examples. If you think you'd like to start volunteering, write down where and how you will. If you want to start attending religious services, write down exactly where and when you'll begin, and so on. Write your ideas here:

Find Your Quiet Within

One of the key components to strengthening your connection with your own spirit and with the universe, God, or whatever higher power you believe is learning how to just *be*. It is inside that quiet stillness that spiritual growth takes place. But today, our lives are loud. We are on information hyperdrive. We have screens flashing at us from every angle. We have people's opinions, ones we don't even ask for, yelled at us. And advertisements, the insidious side effects of this full-fledged consumer age, enter into our consciousness relentlessly and without our permission. Our brains are firing on all cylinders from the moment we open our eyes until we close them again many hours and countless interactions and transactions later. The ultimate antidote to this noisy existence is to draw inward, and reclaim our quiet. Instead of always allowing the world to shape our thoughts and feelings, we must learn through this practice to create peace inside yourself regardless of the outer frenzy.

Maybe you haven't visited your own quiet place in a long time and aren't sure how to get there anymore. I can tell you that the biggest distraction most of us face is technology. So, your first order of business will be to disconnect from tech when you are ready to connect with your quiet place inside. If you're trying to check email, or hearing the alerts on your phone or computer, you're going to have a tougher time with this.

Here are some techniques for rediscovering it so that you can deepen your spiritual experiences and life.

TECHNIQUE 1: Pump Up the Volume, Drown Out the Noise

One of the ways I can easily access my inner quiet—that place where all my other thoughts just melt away, and I feel calm and in alignment—

is to turn on music. It is when I can sync my mind to the rhythm and tune of music that moves me that I'm best able to feel that peace. Does music give you the same feeling?

Try this little experiment:

- Find a time when you have at least ten minutes to yourself.
- Sit down in a relaxed setting where you have a speaker or earphones so you can hear music.
- Play a few different types of music, and see if any one of them puts you into a peaceful state where you feel you can just be, without your mind running at 90 miles per hour, or worries creeping in, etc.
- If you find one, then create time in your schedule to listen to it at least a few minutes a day, and while doing so visit your quiet place.

TECHNIQUE 2: Tap into Nature

Another common way to access inner quiet is to get into an outdoor setting, and let nature help along the process. Whether we realize it or not, our minds and bodies are attuned to the earth in interesting ways, so especially if we spend the majority of our time indoors, it's essential to get outside whenever possible. This might be the easiest way for you to connect with your own quiet place.

There are endless possibilities for outside activities, but here's a list for inspiration:

- **Go on a nature hike**. Don't make it about how far you can walk, how many calories you can burn, or anything other than just feeling as though you are connecting with your natural environment. Notice the trees, grass, rocks, hills, flowers, or anything else around you and just be part of it.
- **Ride a bike** without the express goal of "exercising," but instead, go on a sightseeing tour. Again, look at the natural elements around you—the birds flying overhead, the feel of the terrain under your tires, and so on.
- If you live near a body of water, take a **boat, canoe, or kayak** out. Water can be very soothing, and it can help settle your mind. Listen to the sound of the water as you move through it, and take note of your surroundings.
- Find a quiet place outside, and just **sit down and listen to your own breathing**. Allow your brain to tune in to the buzzing of insects, the chirping of birds, and the breeze blowing through the trees and grass.

TECHNIQUE 3: Get Your Yoga On

The practice of yoga can be good for more than just getting a good stretch. It can be a way for you to connect with your breathing, to really feel your body in a way you can't when you're sitting in a car, or at a desk, or on the couch. Also, we sometimes tend to hold on to or "store" emotional pain in our physical bodies, and yoga is a powerful way to release that pain and begin to move toward healing.

If you've done yoga before, but haven't in a while, I'd encourage you to pick it back up. It doesn't have to be a full hour class, and you don't even have to go anywhere. Yoga is something you can do in the comfort of your own home. There are many videos online that will guide you through the proper form of a certain pose. Choose yoga poses that feel the most relaxing to you, and focus on those.

Staying Accountable

As we discussed earlier in this chapter, community is an essential piece of your spiritual picture. Think about who you have in your life who might be a good fit for keeping you accountable to the work you're doing on a spiritual level. And if you don't have anyone, that's okay! That's even more of a reason to go out and meet people who would be great for this.

My accountability partner for my Spiritual life is:

_____

Next, write down how you will ask this person to help keep you on this new path. Will you ask them to help you say "yes" to new spiritual opportunities? Whatever your plan is, write it down here:

I will ask my accountability partner to help me by:

_____

_____

_____

Tracking Your Progress

After a couple of weeks, return to this chapter and check in with yourself to see if you've kept the forward momentum in your evolution. Do you feel you've made progress? Are there areas that require more of your attention? Write a few lines about how you've noticed yourself improving in your spiritual life.

_____

_____

_____

_____

Before You Go . . .

We've all had days, or maybe even whole seasons, when life has just seemed so complicated. When those times come around, I want you to remember this—you hold the power to simplify things. All you have to do is show up as your Best Self. That's it! You don't need to analyze every thought or emotion you experience, and you certainly don't need to analyze other people in your life. The only person you can control is *you*. And when you approach any situation that arises from your own authenticity, your odds of a positive outcome increase exponentially.

On the other hand, if you behave in a way that you think will bring about a certain outcome, you inevitably run into problems. For instance, if you say or do something because you think it will please someone else, but your behavior is not authentic to who you are—problems. If you lash out at someone because you think they need to be punished or to acknowledge that you're right—problems. And if you set up a dynamic with someone in your life that is based on a version of yourself that isn't your Best Self—more problems. You get the point.

Of course, acting as your Best Self doesn't guarantee that you'll have a life free of adversity, discord, or disagreements. On the contrary! But the difference is this—if you're true to who you are in all of your interactions, then you can move confidently through your life knowing that you don't compromise your core values for anyone or anything. And your Best Self is wise; he or she knows exactly how you should handle whatever comes your way. You just need to trust yourself, and have faith that God or the universe ultimately has your back.

The work you've done in this companion guide has likely been challenging, and made you aware of the work you have to do. That's good. You want to challenge yourself, to discover the answers you have within you. I encourage you to return to this work and to check in with yourself from time to time. We're constantly evolving, and part of that evolution is maintaining a strong connection with your Best Self. But it requires a willingness on your part, as well as a curiosity. We are not innately self-aware beings; our Best Self requires practice and persistence.

There might be times in the future when you start to feel like you've strayed off course in one of your SPHERES. Maybe you're not at all sure why you're struggling within it, and you need some clarity. Use this book as your navigational tool to get back on track. Just flip it open right to that chapter and start working through the questions so that you can see yourself with some objectivity.

Within the Coach Mike social media platforms, you'll find lots of people sharing the epiphanies they've had from reading *Best Self*, and my sincere hope is that you will also engage and share your story. Not only will you feel motivated and empowered, but you will also help others who will relate to your story and struggle. You just might discover the encouragement you were looking for while you're there. I'm not big into putting labels on ourselves, but if you have made it this far, I consider you a "Best Selfer." Welcome to the community.